≈ *Fast Talk*

Swedish

Guaranteed to get you talking

Contents

≡ Special Features

5 Phrases
To Learn Before You Go ... 6

10 Phrases
To Sound Like a Local 7

10 Phrases
To Start a Sentence 8

10 Phrases
To Get You Talking 96

Before You Go

Swedish belongs to the Nordic branch of the Germanic languages. It's spoken by the Swedes, who number close to ten million, and by the Finnish-Swedish minority in southern Finland, including the island of Åland. The language is very closely related to Danish and Norwegian. In fact, Scandinavians can usually make themselves understood in their sister countries.

PRONUNCIATION TIPS

There's a great variety of dialects in Sweden. The pronunciation guide in this book reflects a neutral Swedish, rikssvenska, but don't be surprised if you're given a slightly different pronunciation from a Swede. It all depends on where they come from!

★ It's important to get the stress right in words. Swedish can have a single or a double accent on a word, giving it its sing-song quality, and sometimes the difference of meaning between two identical-looking words can be huge depending on

which accent is used. A good example is glass 'glahss' and glas 'glaas' where the former is 'ice cream' and the latter is 'glass'. In this guide we have used italic letters to denote stressed syllables.

★ Most Swedish sounds are similar to their English counterparts. One exception is fh (a breathy sound pronounced with rounded lips, like saying 'f' and 'w' at the same time), but with a little practice, you'll soon get it right. Note also that ai is pronounced as in 'aisle', aw as in 'saw', air as in 'hair', eu as the 'u' in 'nurse', ew as the 'ee' in 'see' with rounded lips, and ey as the 'e' in 'bet' but longer. Just read our coloured pronunciation guides as if they were English and you'll be understood. The stressed syllables are indicated with italics.

GRAMMAR

You will notice that there are three extra letters in Swedish: å, ä and ö. These are the last three letters of the alphabet, so if you want to look up Åkesson in the telephone directory, you have to look near the end.

SOUNDS FAMILIAR?

Since English and Swedish have common roots in ancient Germanic, there are many similarities between the languages. Many words were also borrowed from Old Norse into the English language during the Viking period, which ended about a thousand years ago, making the language connection even stronger. In modern times the borrowing is going in the opposite direction, with Swedish borrowing mainly from American English.

Fast Talk Swedish

Don't worry if you've never learnt Swedish (svenska svehn-skuh) before – it's all about confidence. You don't need to memorise endless grammatical details or long lists of vocabulary – you just need to start speaking. You have nothing to lose and everything to gain when the locals hear you making an effort. And remember that body language and a sense of humour have a role to play in every culture.

"you just need to start speaking"

Even if you use the very basics, such as greetings and civilities, your travel experience will be the better for it. Once you start, you'll be amazed how many prompts you'll get to help you build on those first words. You'll hear people speaking, pick up sounds and expressions from the locals, catch a word or two that you know from TV already, see something on a billboard – all these things help to build your understanding.

5

Phrases to Learn Before You Go

1. Can I access the Internet from here?
Kan jag koppla upp mig på Internet härifrån?

*ku*hn yuh kop-luh *up* may por *in*-tehrr-neht *haer*-i-*frrorn*

Wireless internet access at coffee shops is nearly universal and usually free.

2. What's the local speciality?
Vad är den lokala specialiteten?

vaad air deyn loh-*kaa*-la spe-si-a-li-*tey*-ten

Scandinavian cuisine, once viewed as meatballs, herring and little else, is now at the forefront of modern gastronomy.

3. I'm looking for a public toilet.
Jag letar efter en offentlig toalett.

yuh *lea*-tuhrr ehf-tehrr ehn oo-*fehnt*-li too-uh-*leht*

Public toilets in parks, shopping malls, libraries, and bus or train stations are rarely free in Sweden.

4. What would you recommend?
Vad skulle ni rekommendera?

vaad *sku*-le nee re-ko-men-*dey*-ra

Let a local recommend a delicious, fresh blast of local flavour.

5. How do you say...?
Hur säger man ...?

hürr say-ehrr muhn ...

Most Swedes speak English, but attempts to speak the local language will be much appreciated.

10. Phrases to Sound Like a Local

| Cool! | **Cool!** | *kool* |

| No worries. | **Inga problem.** | eng-aa proo-*blem* |

| Sure. | **Javisst.** | yuh-vist |

| No way! | **Det menar du inte?** | deh *mea*-narr du *in*-teh |

| Just joking! | **Jag skojar bara!** | yuh sko-yar ba-rah |

| Too bad. | **Vad synd.** | vuh sünd |

| What a shame. | **Vad tråkigt.** | vuh *trro*-kigt |

| What's up? | **Läget?** | *lae*-geht |

| Well done! | **Bra jobbat.** | brrah *jo*-bat |

| Not bad. | **Inte illa.** | en-teh e-lah |

10. Phrases to Start a Sentence

When's (your birthday)?	När fyller du år?
	naer fül-ler du or-rr
Where is (the bus stop)?	Var är (busshållplatsen)?
	vahrr air (bus-hol-pluht-sehn)
Where can I (rent a car)?	Var kan jag (hyra en bil)?
	vahrr kuhn yuh (hü-rruh ehn beel)
Do you have (a map)?	Har ni (en karta)?
	hahrr ni (ehn kah-rtuh)
Is there (a lift)?	Finns det (hiss)?
	fins deh (his)
I'd like (the bill).	Jag skulle vilja (ha notan).
	yaa sku·le vil·ya (haa nooh-tan)
I'd like to (book a seat).	Jag skulle vilja (boka en plats).
	yuh skul-leh vil-yuh (boo-kuh ehn pluhts)
Can I (look at it)?	Får jag (se den)?
	fawr yaa (se deyn)
Do I have to (book)?	Måste man (boka)?
	mos-teh muhn (boo-kuh)
Can you (show me)?	Kan du (visa mig)?
	kuhn du (vee-suh may)

Chatting & Basics

≡ Fast Phrases

Hello.	Hej. *hay*
Goodbye	Adjö!/Hej då! *uh-yer/ hay dor*
Thank you.	Tack. *tuhk*

Essentials

Yes./No.	Ja./Nej. *yah/nay*
Excuse me.	Ursäkta mig. *ü-shehk-tuh may*
May I?	Får jag? *for yuh?*
Do you mind?	Gör det något? *yer-rr deh nor-got*
Sorry.	Förlåt. *fer-lort*
Please.	Tack. *tuhk*
Many thanks.	Tack så mycket. *tuhk sor mü-keh*

Pronunciation

Below is a general pronunciation guide of the sounds that are common to Swedish, outlining in red our representation of each sound, used in the simplified transliterations throughout the book.

Vowels

Most Swedish vowels have a long and a short variant. In a stressed syllable, a vowel is short if it's followed by two consonants and (generally) long when followed by only one consonant. The unstressed syllables have short vowel sounds.

The letter e is always pronounced in Swedish, even at the end of words, and the letter y is always a vowel.

The vowels are divided into two groups, the hard vowels are a, o, u, å and the soft vowels are e, i, y, ä, ö. They help determine the pronunciation of certain preceding consonants.

ah	as the 'a' in 'father'
uh	as the 'u' in 'cut'
a	as the 'a' in 'act'
eh	as the 'e' in 'bet'
ee	as the 'ee' in 'seethe'
i	as the 'i' in 'hit'
ü	a bit like the 'e' in British English 'dew' – try pursing your lips and saying 'ee'
o	a short 'o' as in 'pot'
oh	as the 'o' in 'note'
oo	a long 'oo' as in 'cool'
u	a short 'oo' as in 'foot'
ö	as the 'e' in 'summer'

| or | | as the 'or' in 'for', with less emphasis on the 'r' |
| er | | as the 'er' in 'fern' but shorter, without the 'r' |

Diphthongs

Swedish	Guide	Sounds
e	ea	as in British English 'fear'

Consonants

Some consonants have different sounds depending on whether the following vowel is hard or soft (see Vowels above).

Swedish	Guide	Sounds
g	g	as in 'get' in front of hard vowels and consonants
	y	as in 'yet' in front of soft vowels
j	y	as in 'yet'. This sound can be spelled dj, g, gj, hj, lj at the beginning of words.
k	k	as 'c' in 'cap' in front of hard vowels and consonants
	ch	as tj in front of soft vowels
tj	ch	as the 'ch' in 'cheap' but without the slight 't' sound initially. Can also be spelled ch, k, kj.
sj	fh	not unlike 'sh' in 'ship' but try touching the inside of your lower lip with your front teeth while saying it. Can be spelled ch sch, skj, stj.
sk	fh	in front of soft vowels as sj, in other posi-tions each letter is pronounced separately

That's fine.	Det är bra. *dea air brrah*
You're welcome.	Varsågod. *vuh-sho-goo*

Language Difficulties

Do you speak English?	Talar du engelska? *tah-luhrr du ehng-ehls-kuh*
Does anyone speak English?	Finns det någon här som talar engelska? *fins deh non hair som tah-luhrr ehng-ehls-kuh*
I speak a little Swedish.	Jag talar lite svenska. *yuh tah-luhrr lee-teh svehn-skuh*
I don't speak ...	Jag talar inte ... *yuh tah-luhrr in-teh ...*
I (don't) understand.	Jag förstår (inte). *yuh fer-shtor-rr (in-teh)*
Could you speak more slowly please?	Kan du vara snäll och tala lite långsammare? *kuhn du vuh snehl o tah-luh lee-teh long-suhm-muh-rreh*
Could you repeat that?	Kan du upprepa det? *kuhn doo up-rrea-puh deh*
Could you please write it down?	Skulle du kunna skriva ner det är du snäll? *skuh-le du kunah skrrivah newr deth air du snael?*
How do you say ...?	Hur säger man ...? *hürr say-ehrr muhn ...*
What does that mean?	Vad betyder det? *vuh beh-tü-dehrr dea*

Fast Talk

Starting Off

When starting to speak another language, your biggest hurdle is saying aloud what may seem to be just a bunch of sounds. The best way to do this is to memorise a few key words, like 'hello', 'thank you' and 'how much?', plus at least one phrase that's not essential, eg 'how are you', 'see you later' or 'it's very cold/hot' (people love to talk about the weather!). This will enable you to make contact with the locals, and when you get a reply and a smile, it'll also boost your confidence.

Greetings

Good morning.	Godmorgon.	*goo-mo-rr-on*
Good afternoon.	Godmiddag.	*goo-mid-duh*
Good evening/night.	Godkväll/Godnatt.	*goo-kvehl/goo-nuht*
How are you?	Hur står det till?	*hürr stor rde til*
Well, thanks.	Bra, tack.	*brrah tuhk*

Titles

Mrs	fru	*frrü*
Mr	herr	*harr*
Miss	fröken	*frrer-kehn*

Introductions

What is your name?	Vad heter du? vuh hea-tehrr du
My name is ...	Jag heter ... yuh hea-tehrr ...
I'd like to introduce you to ...	Får jag presentera ... for-rr yuh prreh-sehn-tea-rra ...
I'm pleased to meet you.	Trevligt att träffas./ Angenämt. pol trreav-lit uht trrehf-fuhs/ uhn-yeh-nairmt

PHRASE BUILDER

This is my ...	Detta är mitt/min	De-ta air mit/meen
husband	man	muhn
wife	fru	frrü
child	barn	barn
friend	kompis	kom-pes

Personal Details

Are you married?	Är du gift? air du *yift*
I'm married.	Jag är gift. yuh air *yift*
I'm single.	Jag är ogift. yuh air *ü-yift*
Where are you from?	Varifrån kommer du? *vahrr*-i-frrorn *kom*-mehrr doo

PHRASE BUILDER

I'm from ...	Jag kommer från ...	yuh kom-mehrr frrorn ...
Australia	Australien	uh-u-*strrah*-lee-ehn
Canada	Kanada	*kuh*-nuh-duh
England	England	*ehng*-luhnd
Ireland	Irland	*eer*-luhnd
New Zealand	Nya Zealand	nü-uh *sea*-luhnd
the USA	USA	ü-ehs-*ah*

Age

How old are you?	Hur gammal är du? hürr *guh*-muhl air du
I'm ... years old.	Jag är ... år gammal. yuh air ... or-rr *guh*-mal

Occupations & Study

What is your profession?	Vad har du för yrke? vuh *hahrr* du fer-rr *ürr*-keh
I'm retired.	Jag är pensionerad. yuh air paen-shü-nea-rad

PHRASE BUILDER

I'm (a/an) ...	Jag är ...	yuh air ...
office worker	kontorist	kon-too-*rrist*
student	student	stoo-*dea*-nth
scientist	naturvetare	nuh-*türr*-*vea*-tuh-rreh

15

I'm unemployed.	Jag är arbetslös.
	yuh air ar-behts-luhs
What are you studying?	Vad studerar du?
	vuh stuh-*dae*-rar du

PHRASE BUILDER

I'm studying ...	Jag studerar ...	yuh stuh-*dae*-rar ...
business	ekonomi	ae-koo-no-*mee*
humanities	humaniora	huh-ma-*nyo*-rah
science	naturvetenskap	na-*tuhrr*-vee-teen-*skap*

Interests

What are your interests?	Vad har du för intressen?
	vuh hahrr du fer-rr in-*trrehs*-sehn

PHRASE BUILDER

I (don't) like ...	Jag tycker (inte) om ...	yuh tük-kehrr (*in*-teh) om ...
art	konst	konst
dancing	dans	duhns
music	musik	mu-*seek*
movies	film	film
shopping	att shoppa	uht *shop-puh*
travelling	att resa	uht *rrea-suh*

Feelings

I'm in a hurry.	Jag har bråttom.	yuh hahrr *brrot-tom*
I'm cold.	Jag fryser.	yuh *frrü*-sehrr
I'm well.	Jag mår bra.	yuh mor-rr *brrah*

Numbers

0	noll	nol
1	ett	eht
2	två	tvor
3	tre	trrea
4	fyra	*fü-rruh*
5	fem	fehm
6	sex	sehx
7	sju	fhü
8	åtta	*ot-tuh*
9	nio	*nee-oo*

10	tio	*tee-oo*
11	elva	*ehl-vuh*
12	tolv	tolv
13	tretton	*trreh-ton*
14	fjorton	*fyoo-rton*
15	femton	*fehm-ton*
16	sexton	*sehx-ton*
17	sjutton	*fhu-ton*
18	arton	*ah-rton*
19	nitton	*ni-ton*
20	tjugo	*chü-goo*
21	tjugoett	chü-goo-*eht*
30	trettio	*trreh-ti*
40	fyrtio	*fer-rti*
50	femtio	*fehm-ti*
60	sextio	*sehx-ti*
70	sjuttio	*fhu-ti*
80	åttio	*ot-ti*
90	nittio	*ni-ti*
100	ett hundra	eht *hun-drruh*
1000	ett tusen	eht *tü-sehn*
one million	en miljon	ehn mil-*yoon*
one billion	en miljard	ehn mil-*yahrd*

Time

| What time is it? | Hur mycket är klockan?
hürr *mük-*keh air *klok-kuhn* |
| It's (two) o'clock. | Klockan är (två).
*klo·*kan air (tvaw) |

18

Local Knowledge

What time is it?
Swedes often use the 24-hour system for telling the time.

Half past (one).	Halv (två). (lit: half two)
	halv (tvaw)
At what time...?	Hur dags ...?
	hur daks ...

Days

Monday	måndag	*mon*-duh
Tuesday	tisdag	*tees*-duh
Wednesday	onsdag	*oons*-duh
Thursday	torsdag	*toosh*-rduh
Friday	fredag	*frrea*-duh
Saturday	lördag	*ler*-rduh
Sunday	söndag	*sern*-duh

Months

January	januari	yuh-nu-*ah*-rri
February	februari	feb-rru-*ah*-rri
March	mars	muhsh
April	april	uhp-*rril*
May	maj	muhy
June	juni	*yü*-ni
July	juli	*yü*-li
August	augusti	uh-*gus*-ti
September	september	sehp-*tehm*-behrr

19

October	oktober	ok-*too*-behrr
November	november	noo-*vehm*-behrr
December	december	deh-*sehm*-behrr

Dates

What date is it today?	Vilket datum är det idag? vil-keht *dah*-tum air deh i-*dah*
It's (18 October).	Det är den 18e oktober. deh air dehn *ar*-ton-deh oc-*too*-ber
today	idag i-dah
now	nu nü
yesterday	igår i-gor-rr
last night	igår kväll i-gor-rr kvehl
last week	förra veckan i fer-rruh vehk-kuhn
last year	förra året fer-rruh or-rreht
tomorrow	i morgon i mo-rron

Weather

What's the weather like?	Hur är vädret? hürr air *vaird*-rreht
It's raining.	Det regnar. deh *rrehng-nuhrr*
It's snowing.	Det snöar. deh *sner-uhrr*

It's sunny.	Solen skiner.
	soo-lehn *fee*-nehrr
It's windy.	Det blåser.
	deh *blor*-sehrr

PHRASE BUILDER

It's ...	Det är ...	deh air ...
cloudy	molnigt	*mol*-nit
cold	kallt	*kuhlt*
foggy	dimmigt	*dim*-mit
frosty	frost ute	*frrost* ü-teh
warm	varmt	*vuhrrmt*

Directions

Where is ...?	Var är/ligger ...?
	vahrr *air/lig*-gehrr ...
What is the address?	Vilken adress är det?
	vil-kehn uh-*drrehs air* deh
Could you write the address, please?	Kan du skriva ner adressen, är du snäll?
	kuhn du skrree-vuh nearr uh-drrehs-sehn air duh snael
How do I get to ...?	Hur kommer man till ...?
	hürr *kom*-mehrr muhn til ...

PHRASE BUILDER

Turn left/right at the ...	Sväng till vänster/ höger vid ...	*svehng* til *vehns*-tehrr/ *her*-gehrr veed ...
next	nästa	*nehst*-uh
corner	hörn	*her*-rn
traffic lights	trafikljuset	trruh-*feek-yü*-seht

Is it near here?	Är det långt härifrån?
	air deh longt haer-i-frrorn
Can I walk there?	Kan man gå dit?
	kuhn muhn gor deet
Can you show me (on the map)?	Kan du visa mig (på kartan)?
	kuhn du vee-suh may (po kah-rtuhn)
Are there other means of getting there?	Kan jag komma dit på annat sätt?
	kuhn muhn kom-muh deet po uhn-nuht seht
Go straight ahead.	Gå rakt fram.
	gor rrahkt frruhm
behind	bakom
	bah-kom
in front of	framför
	frruhm-fer-rr
far	långt
	longt
near	nära
	nae-rruh
opposite	mitt emot
	mit eh-moot

Airport & Transport

≡ Fast Phrases

What time is the next bus?	När går nästa buss? naer gor-rr *nehs*-ta *bus*
Which line takes me to ...?	Vilken linje går till ...? vil-kehn *leen*-yeh gor-rr til ...
I'd like a one-way ticket.	Jag skulle vilja ha en enkel-biljett. yuh *skul*-leh vil-yuh *hah* ehn *ehn*-kehl-bil-*yeht*

At the Airport

Is there a flight to ...?	Finns det något flyg till ...? fins deh not *flüg* til ...
How long does the flight take?.	Hur lång tid tar flyget? hürr long teed *tahrr* *flü*-geht
What is the flight number?	Vilket flightnummer är det? vil-keht *flight-num*-mehrr *air* deh
I'm not sure how long I'm staying.	Jag vet inte hur länge jag stannar. yuh *veat* in-teh hurr *lehng*-eh yuh *stuhn*-uhrr

23

🔍 LOOK FOR

ANKOMST	**ARRIVALS**
AVGÅNG	**DEPARTURES**
BAGAGEUTLÄMNING	**LUGGAGE PICKUP**
BILJETTKONTOR	**TICKET OFFICE**
BUSSHÅLLPLATS	**BUS STOP**
FLYGBUSS	**AIRPORT BUS**
JÄRNVÄGSSTATION	**TRAIN STATION**
PASSKONTROLL	**IMMIGRATION**
SPÅR	**PLATFORM**
SPÅRVAGNSHÅLLPLATS	**TRAM STOP**
TIDTABELL	**TIMETABLE**
TUNNELBANA	**SUBWAY**

Getting Around

How long does the trip take?	Hur lång tid tar resan? hurr long *teed tuhrr rrea*-suhn
Is it a direct route?	Är det en direktförbindelse? air deh ehn di-*rrehkt-fer-rr-bin*-dehl-seh

Buying Tickets

Where can I buy a ticket?	Var kan jag köpa en biljett? *vahrr* kuhn yuh *ker*-puh ehn bil-*yeht*
I want to go to ...	Jag vill åka till ... yuh vil *or*-kuh til ...
Do I need to book?	Måste man boka? *mos*-teh muhn *boo-kuh*

PHRASE BUILDER

What time does the ... leave/arrive?	Hur dags går/ kommer ...?	hürr duhks gor-rr/ kom-mehrr ...?
(aero)plane	(flyg)planet	(flüg-)plah-neht
boat	båten	bor-tehn
bus	bussen	bu-sehn
ferry	färjan	farr-yuhn
train	tåget	tor-geht
tram	spårvagnen	spor-rr-vuhng-nehn

What time is the next bus?	När går nästa buss? near gor-rr nehs-ta bus
What time is the first bus?	När går första bussen? near gor-rr fersh-tuh bu-sehn
What time is the last bus?	När går sista bussen? near gor-rr sis-tuh bu-sehn

PHRASE BUILDER

I'd like (a) ...	Jag skulle vilja ha ...	yuh skul-leh vil-yuh hah ...
one-way ticket	en enkelbiljett	ehn ehn-kehl-bil-yeht
return ticket	en returbiljett	ehn rreh-türr-bil-yeht
two tickets	två biljetter	tvor bil-yeht-ehrr
student's fare	en studentbiljett	ehn stu-dehnt-bil-yeht
child's fare	en barnbiljett	ehn bahrn-bil-yeht
pensioner's fare	en pensionärs-biljett	puhn-fhoo-naesh-bil-yeht

I'd like to book a seat to ...	Jag skulle vilja boka en plats till ... yuh *skul*-leh vil-yuh *boo*-kuh ehn *pluhts* til ...

PHRASE BUILDER

I'd like a/an ... seat.	Jag skulle vilja ha ett säte vid...	yuh skul-leh vil-yuh hah eht saeteh ved...
aisle	gång	gohng
(non)smoking	rökfri	rruhk-free
window	fönster	fuhn-stehrr

Luggage

I'd like a luggage locker.	Jag skulle vilja ha bagageförvaring. yuh skuh-le *vil*-yuh haw ba-*gach*-fer-varing
Can I have some coins/ tokens?	Skulle jag kunna få några mynt? skuh-le yuh *kuh*-nah fo no-grah münt

PHRASE BUILDER

My luggage has been ...	Mitt bagage har blivit ...	mit ba-gach hahrr blee-vit ...
damaged	skadat	*skah*-daht
lost	borttappat	*boort*-ta-paht
stolen	stulet	*stuh*-leth

Bus & Train

I want to get off at ...	Jag vill gå av i ... *yuh vil gor ahv ee ...*
Is that seat taken?	Är det upptaget här? *air deh up-tah-geht haer*
Where is the bus/tram stop?	Var är busshållplatsen/ spårvagnshållplatsen? *vahrr air bus-hol-pluht-sehn/ spor-rr-vuhngns-hol-pluht-sehn*
Which bus goes to ...?	Vilken buss går till ...? *vil-kehn bus gor-rr til ...*
Does it stop at (Lund)?	Stannar den i (Lund)? *sta·nar den ee (lund)*
Could you let me know when we get to ...?	Kan du säga till när vi kommer till ...? *kuhn du seh-ya til naer vi kom-mehrr til ...*
Which line takes me to ...?	Vilken linje går till ...? *vil-kehn leen-yeh gor-rr til ...*
What is the next station?	Vilken är nästa station? *vil-kehn air nehs-tuh stuh-fhoon*
I want to get off!	Jag vill gå av! *yuh vil gor ahv*
Is this the right platform for the train to/from ...?	Är det här rätt perrong för tåget till/från ...? *air deh haer rreht pa-rrong fer-rr tor-geht til/frrorn ...*
Is this the train to (Stockholm)?	Är det här tåget till (Stockholm)? *air de hair taw-get til (stok-holm)*
Passengers for ... must change trains in ...	Resande mot ... måste byta tåg i ... *rrea-suhn-deh moot ... mos-teh bü tuh torg i ...*

🔍 LOOK FOR

RESTURANGVAGN	**DINING CAR**
EXPRESSTÅG	**EXPRESS**
LOKALTÅG	**LOCAL**
SOVVAGN	**SLEEPING CAR**

The train leaves from platform ...	Tåget avgår från spår ... *torg*-eht *ahv-gor-rr* frrorn *spor-rr* ...
The train is delayed/ cancelled.	Tåget är försenat/inställt. *tor*-geht air fer-*shea*-nuht/*in-stehlt*
How long will it be delayed?	Hur mycket är det försenat? hurr *mük-keh* air deh fer-*shea*-nuht

Taxi

Where's the taxi stand?	Var är taxihållplatsen? Vahrr air taxi-hol-platsen
I'd like a taxi at (9am).	Jag skulle vilja beställa en taxi till klockan nio på morgonen. yuh skuh-le *vil*-yuh beh-*ste*-lah ein taxi tel kloh-kuhn neo paw mor-go-nehn
Can you take me to ...?	Kan du köra mig till ...? kuhn doo *cher*-rruh may til ...
Please take me to this address.	Kan du köra mig till denna address? kan doo sheu·ra mey til
How much does it cost to go to ...?	Vad kostar det till ...? vuh *kos*-tuhrr deh til dey·na a·dres

Here is fine, thank you.	Här blir bra, tack.
	haer bleer *brrah* tuhk
Stop here!	Stanna här!
	stuhn-uh *haer*
The next corner, please.	Nästa hörn, tack.
	nehs-tuh *her-rn* tuhk
Continue!	Fortsätt!
	foort-sheht
Please slow down.	Kan du sakta ner?
	kuhn du suhk-tuh *nearr*
Please wait here.	Kan du vänta här?
	kuhn du *vehn*-tuh *haer*

Car & Motorcycle

Where can I rent a car?	Var kan jag hyra en bil?
	vahrr kuhn yuh *hü-*rruh ehn beel
I'd like to hire a motorcycle.	Jag vill hyra en motorcykel.
	yaa vil *hew·*ra eyn *moh·*tor-sew·kel
How much is it daily/weekly?	Hur mycket kostar det per dag/per vecka?
	hurr mük-keh kos-tuhrr deh parr *dahg*/parr *vehk-kuh*
Does that include insurance/mileage?	Ingår försäkring/fria mil?
	in-gor-rr fer-*shaek-*rring/*frree-uh* meel
Does this road lead to?	Går den här vägen till ...?
	gor-rr dehn *haer* vair-gehn til ...
Where's the next petrol station?	Var är nästa bensinstation?
	vahrr air *nehs-*tuh behn-*seen-*stuh-*fhoon*

Fast Talk

How Far?

In Sweden, all road signs show distance in kilometres, but the Swedes prefer to use the term mil (meel) for 10 km when they talk about how far away a place is, eg 50 km is fem mil.

How long can I park here?	Hur länge får man parkera här? hurr *lehng*-eh for-rr muhn puhrr-*kea*-rruh haer
Is this the road to (Göteborg)?	Går den här vägen till (Göteborg)? gawr den hair *vey*-gen til (yeu·te·*bory*)

Cycling

Where can I hire a bicycle?	Var kan jag hyra en cykel? vahrr kuhn yuh *hü*-rruh ehn *sük*-kehl
Are there cycling paths?	Finns det cykelvägar? fens deth *sü*-kehl-*vae*-gar
Is there bicycle parking?	Finns det cykelparkering? fens deth *sü*-kehl-par-*ke*-ring

Accommodation

≋ Fast Phrases

I have a reservation.	Jag har bokat. yuh hahr *boo*-kat
When/Where is breakfast served?	Var serverar man frukost? vahrr sehr-veh-rar mahn *frroo*-kost
What time is checkout?	När är utcheckningen? Naer air uht-check-ni-ngehn

Finding Accommodation

What is the address?	Vilken adress är det? vil-kehn uh-*drrehs* air deh
Could you write the address, please?	Kan du skriva ner adressen, tack? kuhn du skrree-vuh *nearr* uh-*drrehs*-sehn tuhk

PHRASE BUILDER

Where is a ... hotel?	Var finns det ett ... hotell?	vahrr *fins* deh eht ... hoo-*tehl*
cheap	billigt	*bil*-lit
good	bra	*brrah*
nearby	närliggande	*naer*-lig-guhn-deh

Hotels

Can you recommend somewhere cheap?	Skulle du kunna rekommendera något billigt? *skul*-leh du ku-nah re-ko-men-*dey*-ra noh-goht bel-lehgt
Can you recommend somewhere nearby?	Skulle du kunna rekommendera något nära? *skul*-leh du ku-nah re-ko-men-*dey*-ra noh-goht naerah
Can you recommend somewhere romantic?	Skulle du kunna rekommendera något romantiskt? *skul*-leh du ku-nah re-ko-men-*dey*-ra noh-goht roh-mahn-tiskt

Booking & Checking In

I have a reservation.	Jag har bokat. yuh hahr boo-kat
Do you have any rooms available?	Finns det några lediga rum? *fins* deh nor-grruh *lea*-di-guh *rrum*
I'd like to share a dorm.	Jag skulle vilja bo i sovsal. yuh *skul*-leh vil-yuh *boo* ee *sorv*-sahl

PHRASE BUILDER

I'd like a ...	Jag skulle vilja ha ...	yuh *skul*-leh vil-yuh *hah* ...
single room	ett enkelrum	eht *ehn*-kehl-*rrum*
double room	ett dubbelrum	eht *dub*-behl-*rrum*
bed	en säng	ehn *sehng*

PHRASE BUILDER

I want a room with a ...	Jag vill ha ett rum med ...	yuh vil *hah* eht *rrum* meh ...
balcony	balkong	buhl-*kong*
bathroom	badrum	bahd-room
shower	dusch	dufh
television	TV	*tea-vea*
window	fönster	*fern*-stehrr

How much is it per night/per person?	Hur mycket kostar det per natt/per person? hurr mük-keh *kos*-tuhrr deh parr *nuht*/parr pa-*shoon*
I'm going to stay for one day.	Jag tänker stanna en dag. yuh tehn-kehrr *stuhn-nuh ehn dah*
I'm going to stay for one week.	Jag tänker stanna en vecka. yuh tehn-kehrr *stuhn-nuh ehn veh-kuh*
I'm not sure how long I'm staying.	Jag vet inte hur länge jag stannar. yuh *veat* in-teh hurr *lehng*-eh yuh *stuhn*-uhrr

🔍 LOOK FOR

CAMPINGPLATS	CAMPING GROUND
FULLBELAGT/INGA LEDIGA RUM	FULL/NO VACANCIES
GÄSTGIVERI/PENSIONAT	GUESTHOUSE
HOTELL	HOTEL
MOTELL	MOTEL
LEDIGA RUM/RUM ATT HYRA	ROOMS AVAILABLE
VANDRARHEM	YOUTH HOSTEL

33

Are there any other/ cheaper rooms?	Finns det några andra/ billigare rum? *fins deh nor-grruh uhnd-rruh/ bil-li-guh-rreh rrum*
Does it include breakfast?	Ingår frukost i priset? *in-gor-rr frru-kost i prree-seht*
Can I see the room?	Kan jag få se rummet? *kuhn yuh for sea rrum-meht*
It's fine, I'll take it.	Det blir bra, jag tar det. *deht bleer brrah yuh tahrr deh*
I'd like to pay the bill.	Jag skulle vilja betala räkningen. *yuh skul-leh vil-yuh beh-tah-luh rrairk-ning-ehn*

Requests & Questions

Please wake me up at ...	Kan ni väcka mig klockan ...? *kuhn ni vehk-kuh may klok-kuhn ...*
Do you have a safe where I can leave my valuables?	Har ni någon förvaringsbox där jag kan lämna mina värdesaker? *hahrr ni non fer-rr-vah-rrings-boks daer yuh kuhn lehm-nuh mee-nuh vaer-deh-sah-kehrr*
Is there somewhere to wash clothes?	Finns det någon tvättstuga? *fins deh non tveht-stü-guh*
Is there a lift?	Finns det hiss? *fins deh his*
Can I use the kitchen?	Kan jag använda köket? *kuhn yuh uhn-vehn-duh ker-keht*
May I use the telephone?	Får jag låna telefonen? *for-rr yuh lor-nuh teh-leh-for-nehn*

Fast Talk

Using Patterns

Look out for patterns of words or phrases that stay the same, even when the situation changes, eg 'Do you have ...?' or 'I'd like to ...'. If you can recognise these patterns, you're already halfway there to creating a full phrase. The dictionary will help you put other words together with these patterns to convey your meaning – even if it's not completely grammatically correct in all contexts, the dictionary form will always be understood.

Complaints

I (don't) like this room.	Jag tycker inte om det här rummet.	
	yuh tük-kehrr (in-teh) om deh haer rrum-meht	
The room needs to be cleaned.	Rummet behöver städas.	
	rrum-meht beh-her-vehrr stair-duhs	
I can't open/close the window.	Jag kan inte öppna/stänga fönstret.	
	yuh kuhn in-teh erp-nuh/stehng-uh fernst-rreht	
I've locked myself out of my room.	Jag har låst mig ute.	
	yuh hahrr lorst may ü-teh	

PHRASE BUILDER

It's too ...	Det är för ...	deh air fer-rr ...
dark	mörkt	*mer-rrkt*
expensive	dyrt	*dürt*
noisy	bullrigt	*bul-rrit*
small	litet	*lee-teht*

The toilet won't flush.	Toaletten spolar inte. too-uh-*leht*-tehn *spoo*-luhrr *in*-teh

Checking Out

What time is checkout?	När är utcheckningen? naer air uht-check-ni-ngehn
Can I leave my bags here?	Skulle jag kunna få lämna mitt bagage här? skul-leh yuh ku-nah fo laem-nah mit ba-gach hear

PHRASE BUILDER

Could I have my ..., please?	Skulle jag kunna få...är du snäll?	skul-leh yuh *ku*-nah fo... air du snael
deposit	deposition	deh-poh-*see*-fhün
passport	pass	puhs
valuables	värdesaker	vaer-dee-sah-kerr

Useful Words

address	uh-*drrehs*	adress
room number	*rrums*-num-mehrr	rumsnummer
air-conditioning	*luft*-kon-di-fhoo-*nea*-rring	luftkonditionering
balcony	buhl-*kong*	balkong
bathroom	*bahd*-room	badrum
bed	sehng	säng
blanket	filt	filt
double bed	*dub*-behl-*sehng*	dubbelsäng

In the Country

Sweden offers unique possibilities for trekking, canoeing and camping as Allemansrätten 'Everyman's right' allows you to use all land, regardless of ownership, as long as you are careful and don't cause any damage or bother the owner. You can even pitch a tent for one night without permission, but for a caravan or a longer stay, ask the land owner first. And remember to clean up before you leave!

fan	flehkt	fläkt
heater	*varr*-meh-eh-leh-*mehnt*	värmeelement
key	*nük-kehl*	nyckel
lift (elevator)	hiss	hiss
pillow	*kud-deh*	kudde
suitcase	*rreas-vehs-*kuh	resväska
swimming pool	*sim-*buh-*sehng*	simbassäng
towel	*huhn-dook*	handduk

Camping

Am I allowed to camp here?	Får jag campa här? for-rr yuh *kuhm*-puh *haer*
Is there a campsite nearby?	Finns det någon campingplats i närheten? fins deh non *kuhm*-ping-*pluhts* ee *naer-hea-*tehn

37

Eating & Drinking

≡ Fast Phrases

Can I see the menu, please?	Kan jag få se menyn? kuhn yuh for sea meh-nün
I'd like to pay the bill.	Jag skulle vilja betala notan. yuh skul-leh vil-yuh beh-tah-luh noo-tahn
Table for ..., please.	Ett bord för ..., tack! eht *bord* fer-rr ... tuhk

Meals

breakfast	frukost *frroo*-kost
lunch	lunch lunfh
dinner	middag *mid*-duh
supper	kvällsmat kvaels-maht
dessert	dessert dehs-*saer*

Local Knowledge

Restaurants

Where would you go for a celebration?	Var skulle du gå för att fira? vahrr skul-leh du go ffer at *fee*-rah
Where would you go for a cheap meal?	Var skulle du gå för att äta billigt? Vahrr skul-leh du go ffer at *ae*-tah bee-ligt
Where would you go for local specialities?	Var skulle du gå för att äta lokala specialiteter? vahrr skul-leh du go ffer at *ae*-tah loh-*kaa*-la spe-si-a-li-tey-terr

Finding a Place to Eat

Are you still serving food?	Serverar ni fortfarande mat? Sehr-*veh*-rar ne fort-fah-ran-deh maht
How long is the wait?	Hur lång är väntetiden? Huhr long air *vaen*-teh-tee-dehn

PHRASE BUILDER

Can you recommend a ...?	Skulle du kunna rekommendera en/ett...?	skul-leh du ku-nah re-ko-men-*dey*-ra ein/eht ...
bar	bar	bar
cafe	kafé	ka·*fey*
restaurant	restaurang	res·taw·*rang*

39

Fast Talk

A Swedish Buffet

The Swedish smörgåsbord is famous throughout the world for its great variety of cold and hot dishes, but there's more to Swedish food than that. Many dishes are associated with different seasons and may be difficult to find at other times.

I'd like to reserve a table for (eight o'clock), please.	Jag skulle gärna vilja boka ett bord till klockan åtta tack. yuh skul-leh yaer-na vil-yuh booka eht boord til *klo*-kan *oh*-ta tuhk
Table for ..., please.	Ett bord för ..., tack! eht *boord* fer-rr ... tuhk

PHRASE BUILDER

I'd like (the) ...	Jag skulle vilja ha ...	yaa sku·le vil·ya haa ...
drink list	drickslistan	*driks*·lis·tan
menu	menyn	me·*newn*
that dish	den maträtten	deyn *maat*·reten
bill	notan	noo·tahn

Ordering & Paying

What would you recommend?	Vad skulle ni rekommendera? vaad *sku*·le nee *re* ko men *dey* ra
What's the local speciality?	Vad är den lokala specialiteten? vaad air deyn loh·*kaa*·la spe·si·a·li·*tey*·ten

I'd like to pay the bill.	Jag skulle vilja betala notan. yuh *skul*-leh vil-yuh beh-*tah*-luh noo-tahn
What does it include?	Vad ingår i det? vuh *in-gor-rr* i *dea*
Is service included in the bill?	Är serveringsavgiften inräknad? air sehrr-*vea*-rrings-ahv-*yif-tehn* in-*rraek*-nuhd
There's a mistake in the bill.	Det är ett fel på räkningen. de air et fel paw *reyk*·ning·en

Special Diets & Allergies

I'm a vegetarian.	Jag är vegetarian. yuh air veh-geh-tuh-rri-*ahn*
I don't eat meat.	Jag äter inte kött. yuh *ae*-tehrr *in*-teh *chert*
I don't eat chicken, or fish, or ham.	Jag äter varken kyckling eller fisk eller skinka yuh *ae*-tehrr *vuhrr*-kehn *chük*-ling ehl-lehrr *fisk* ehl-lehrr *fhing*-kuh

PHRASE BUILDER

I'm allergic to ...	Jag är allergisk mot ...	yuh aer a-*ler*-gisk mot
dairy produce	laktos	lak-*tos*
gluten	gluten	*glu*-ten
MSG	MSG	em-es-g
nuts	nötter	*nu*-terr
seafood	fisk och skaldjur	fesk ohk *skal*-yuhrr
shellfish	skaldjur	*skal*-yuhrr

41

Do you have vegetarian food?	Har ni vegetarisk mat?
	har nee ve·ge·*taa*·risk maat

PHRASE BUILDER

Could you prepare a meal without ...?	Kan ni laga en maträtt utan ...?	kan nee *laa*·ga eyn *maat*·ret oo·tan
butter	smör	smeur
eggs	ägg	eg
meat stock	köttspad	*sheut*·spaad

Non-alcoholic Drinks

coffee	kaffe
	kuh-feh
tea	te
	tea
hot chocolate	varm choklad
	vuhrrm fhook-*lahd*

LOOK FOR

BARNMENY	CHILDREN'S MENU
DAGENS RÄTT	DAILY SPECIAL
ÖPPET	OPEN
STÄNGT	CLOSED
TORGHANDEL	MARKET
MATAFFÄR	SUPERMARKET
GRÖNSAKSAFFÄR	VEGETABLE SHOP
DELIKATESSAFFÄR	DELICATESSEN

Fast Talk

Practising Swedish

If you want to practise your language skills, try the waiters at a restaurant. Find your feet with straight-forward phrases such as asking for a table and ordering a drink, then initiate a conversation by asking for menu recommendations or asking how a dish is cooked. And as you'll often know food terms even before you've 'officially' learnt a word of the language, you're already halfway to understanding the response.

milk	mjölk
	myerlk
orange juice	apelsinjuice
	uh-pehl-seen-yoos
soft drink (carbonated)	läsk
	lehsk
mineral water	mineralvatten
	mi·ne·raal·va·ten
water	vatten
	va-tehn

Alcoholic Drinks

beer	öl/pilsner
	erl/pils-nehrr
fortified wine	starkvin
	stuhrrk-veen
liqueur	likör
	li-ker-rr
red/white wine	rödvin; vitt vin
	rud-veen; vit veen
sparkling wine	mousserande vin
	moo·sey·ran·de veen

I'd like (a beer), please.	Jag skulle vilja ha en öl tack. yuh skul-leh vil-yuh hah ein erl tuhk.
I'll have ...	Jag vill ha ... yaa vil haa ...
Cheers!	Skål! skawl

Buying Food

| What's the local speciality? | Vad är den lokala specialiteten? vaad air deyn loh-kaa-la spe-si-a-li-tey-ten |
| How much is it? | Hur mycket kostar det? hurr mük-keh kos-tuhrr deh? |

Vegetables

asparagus	sparris	*spuhrr*-rris
beans	bönor; haricot vert	*ber-ner*; huh-rri-koo-*vaer*
carrot	morot	*moo-rroot*
lettuce	sallad	*suhl*-luhd
mushrooms	svamp/ champinjoner	svuhmp/ fham-pin-*yoo*-nehrr
onion	lök	lerk
peas	ärtor	*a*-rtehrr
potato	potatis	poo-*tah*-tis
tomato	tomat	too-*maht*
turnip	kålrot	*korl*-rroot

Summer Specialities

During summer the Swedes eat light food, with many cold meals like salads and smoked ham, lots of fish and for dessert a variety of berries (bär) with cream (grädde) or ice cream (glass).

During the Midsummer celebrations, inlagd sill (pickled herring) with sour cream and chives and new potatoes boiled with dill is a must and it's accompanied by a cold beer and a snaps (shot of akvavit) or two. Jordgubbar (strawberries) are most likely served as dessert. Ideally, this meal should be eaten outdoors.

Fruit & Berries

apple	äpple	*ehp-leh*
banana	banan	buh-*nahn*
blackberries	björnbär	*bjer-rn*-baer
grapes	vindruvor	*veen*-drrü-*ver*
lingonberries	lingon	*ling-on*
orange	apelsin	uh-pehl-*seen*
pear	päron	*pae-rron*
plum	plommon	*ploo-mon*
raspberries	hallon	*huhl-lon*
rhubarb	rabarber	rruh-*buhrr*-behrr
strawberries	jordgubbar	*yoord-gub*-buhrr
wild strawberries	smultron	*smult-rron*

Breakfast Menu

bread	bröd	brrerd
bread roll	småfranska/ frukostbulle	*smor-frruhns-kuh/ frru*-kost-*bul*-leh
butter	smör	smer-rr
boiled egg	kokt ägg	*kookt ehg*
cereal	flingor/müsli	*fling-er/müs*-li
cheese	ost	oost
coffee	kaffe	*kuh-feh*
fried egg	stekt ägg	*steakt ehg*
jam	sylt	sült
marmalade	marmelad	muhrr-meh-*lahd*
scrambled eggs	omelett	oo-meh-*leht*
sugar	socker	*sok*-kehrr
toast	rostat bröd	rros-tuht *brrerd*
yoghurt	yoghurt	*yorg*-urt

Meat

beef	nötkött	*nert-chert*
chicken	kyckling	*chük-ling*
ham	skinka	*fhing-kuh*
lamb chops	lammkotletter	*luhm*-kot-*leht*-tehrr
liver paté	leverpastej	*lea*-vehrr-puhs-*tehy*
meatballs	köttbullar	*chert-bul*-luhrr
pork (lean)	griskött	*grrees-chert*
pork (with fat)	fläsk	*flehsk*
sausage/salami	korv/salami	ko-rrv/suh-*lah*-mi

spare ribs	revbensspjäll	*rreav*-beans-*spyehl*
steak	biff/entrecote	bif/uhn-trreh-*kor*
turkey	kalkon	kuhl-*koon*
veal	kalvkött	*kuhlv-chert*

Fish

baltic herring	strömming	*strrer-ming*
cod (roe)	torsk(rom)	*toshk(-rrom)*
crab	krabba	*krruhb-buh*
crayfish	kräftor	*krrehf-ter*
haddock	kolja	*kol-yuh*
halibut	hälleflundra/ helgeflundra	*hehl-leh-flund-rruh*
herring	sill	sil
mackerel	makrill	*muhk-rril*
mussels	musslor	*mus-ler*
prawns	havskräftor	*huhfs-krrehf-ter*
salmon	lax	luhks
shrimps	räkor	*rrair-ker*
sole	sjötunga	*fher-tung-uh*
trout	forell	fo-*rrehl*
whiting	vitling	*vit-ling*

Desserts

| apple pie | äppelpaj | *ehp-pehl-puhy* |
| cake (with cream) | tårta med grädde | *tor-rtuh* mehd graedeh |

cake (no cream)	kaka	*kah*-kuh
cheese cake	ostkaka	*oost-kah*-kuh
mouse	mousse	mous
custard	vaniljkräm/ maizena	vuh-*nily-krrairm*/ muhy-*sea-nuh*
ice cream	glass	gluhs
pancakes	pannkakor/ plättar	*puhn-kah*-ker/ *pleht-tuhrr*

Menu Decoder

This miniguide to Swedish cuisine is designed to help you navigate menus.

Breakfast

filmjölk *feel-myerlk* cultured milk, similar to buttermilk, eaten with cereal and a sprinkle of sugar
gröt *grrert* porridge made of rolled oats
knäckebröd *knehk-keh-brrerd* crisp bread, usually rye
välling *vehl-ling* gruel (Try it, you'll like it!)

Breads and Sandwiches

tunnbröd *tun-brrerd* very thin crisp or soft bread made from barley
vörtbröd *verrt-brrerd* rye bread flavoured with wort (a kind of herb)
franskbröd *frruhnsk-brrerd* white French loaf
fullkornsbröd *ful-koonsh-brrerd* whole grain loaf
grahamsbulle *grrah-huhms-bul-leh* brown bread roll
kavring *kahv-rring* dark sweetened rye bread
limpa *lim-puh* loaf of bread
rågbröd *rrorg-brrerd* rye bread
sötlimpa *sert-lim-puh* sweetened brown loaf

Swedish sandwiches are always open and if they're very elaborate you eat them with a knife and fork. In winter you may be served grilled open sandwiches, varma smörgåsar, for an evening snack. You can make a smörgås with any sort of bread, a thin spread of butter and some pålägg (any kind of sandwich topping).

landgång 'gangplank' – long gourmet sandwich with a variety of pålägg

49

räksmörgås shrimps on lettuce, hardboiled egg, mayonnaise and lemon
sillsmörgås pickled herring on cold boiled potato
smörgåstårta a large layered sandwich with lots of different fillings, cut like a cake

Soup

kålsoppa med frikadeller *korl-sohp*-puh meh frri-kuh-*dehl*-lehrr cabbage soup with boiled meatballs (usually pork)
köttsoppa *chert-sop*-puh beef broth with meat and vegetables
nässelsoppa *neh*-sehl-*sop*-puh nettle soup with a hardboiled egg (spring only)
ärtsoppa *art-sop*-puh yellow pea soup with pork

Meat

Meat is quite expensive in Sweden and the Swedes have come up with a host of different ways of making a little meat go a long way. Casseroles are common, as are dishes made with minced meat like köttbullar (Swedish meatballs), but perhaps the most famous Swedish meat product is the sausage, korv, which comes in all shapes and forms.

biff á la Lindström bif uh-luh *lin-strrerm* patties of minced meat mixed with beetroot and served with a fried egg
blodpudding med lingon *blood-pud*-ding meh *ling-on* black pudding with lingonberry jam
bruna bönor och fläsk brrü-nuh *ber*-ner o *flehsk* brown beans in a sweet sauce with bacon
falukorv *fah*-lu-*ko-rrv* a lean sausage cut in thick slices and fried
isterband is-tehrr-*buhnd* sausage of pork, beef and barley grains
kalops kuh-*lops* meat casserole with onions and allspice
pannbiff med lök *puhn-bif* meh *lerk* minced beef patties with lots of fried onion
pytt i panna püt-i-*puhn-nuh* diced meat, boiled potatoes and onion fried and served with beetroot and a fried egg
rotmos och fläskkorv *rroot-moos* o *flehsk-ko-rrv* boiled pork sausage with mashed turnips

MENU DECODER

varm korv *vuhrrm ko-rrv* hot dog on a breadroll, the special comes with mashed potatoes – Swedish fast food!
viltgryta *vilt-grrü-tuh* game casserole – try älg, elk, in October
kåldolmar *korl-dol-muhrr* stuffed cabbage leaves
lövbiff *lerv-bif* very thinly sliced beef
renskav *rrean-skahv* thinly sliced reindeer meat

Fish & Seafood

Sweden has an enormous coastline and thousands of lakes and fish is an important part of the diet. Kräftor (crayfish) are caught in creeks and lakes from late August and many other types of seafood are brought ashore all year round.

inlagd sill *in-luhgd sil* pickled herring which comes in a great number of varieties
lutfisk *lüt-fisk* dried ling soaked in lye before being boiled. Served with a white sauce with allspice. (Christmas only)
sotare *soo-tuh-rreh* 'chimney sweep' – lightly salted herring grilled over an open fire
böckling *berk-ling* smoked herring
gravad lax *grrah-*vuhd *luhks* cured salmon

Potatoes

Swedes eat potatoes with just about everything and there's a great number of ways to prepare them for the table.

Janssons frestelse *yahn-*sons *frrehs-tehl-seh* 'Jansson's Temptation' – potato, onion and anchovy, oven-baked with lots of cream
raggmunkar/rårakor *rruhg-mung-*kuhrr*/rror-rrah-*ker pancakes made from grated potatoes
råstekt potatis *rror-steakt* poo-*tah-*tis raw potato slices fried in oil
skalpotatis *skahl-*poo-*tah-*tis potatoes boiled in their jackets
stekt potatis *steakt* poo-*tah-*tis fried pre-boiled potatoes
stuvad potatis *stü-*vuhd poo-*tah-*tis potatoes in white sauce
potatismos poo-*tah-*tis-moos mashed potatoes
potatissallad poo-*tah-*tis-*suhl-*luhd potato salad
färskpotatis *fashk-*poo-*tah-*tis new potatoes

Desserts & Pastries

chokladpudding fhook-*lahd*-pud-ding chocolate mousse
kanelbulle kuh-*neal*-*bul*-leh sweet roll with cinnamon and cardamon
kräm och mjölk krrairm-o-*myerlk* thickened berry juice with milk
mazarin muh-suh-*rreen* pastry with almond paste filling
nyponsoppa nü-pon-*sop*-puh rose hip soup, eaten with a dollop of cream
prinsesstårta prrin-*sehs*-tor-rtuh layered sponge cake with jam, cream and custard filling covered with green marzipan
ris á la malta rrees uh-luh *muhl*-tuh rice with whipped cream and orange
schwartzwaldstårta shvuhrtsh-vuhlds-*tor*-rtuh meringue, cream and chocolate cake
småländsk ostkaka smor-lehnsk oost-*kah*-kuh baked curd cake with almonds
sockerkaka sok-kehrr-*kah*-kuh sponge cake, usually flavoured with lemon
skorpor skohrr-*per* rusks
småkakor smor-*kah*-ker biscuits/cookies
wienerbröd vee-nehrr-*brrerd* Danish pastries

Alcoholic Drinks

Alcohol can only be purchased by those over 20 at special shops called Systembolaget. If a Swede asks you if you would like 'a drink', they probably have alcohol in mind as the word drink in Swedish denotes an alcoholic drink, usually a cocktail.

brännvin *brrehn*-veen spirit distilled from potatoes, may be flavoured with herbs and berries or plain
glögg glerg mulled wine with raisins and almonds, served at Christmas
punsch punfh a sweet liqueur flavoured with arrack
snaps snuhps a shot of brännvin. With the word Skål! a shot glass is emptied in one go.
vinbål veen-*borl* a punch based on wine

Sightseeing

≡ Fast Phrases

What time does it open?	När öppnar de? *narr erp-nuhrr dom*
When's the next tour?	När är nästa rundvandring? *near aer nehs-ta rühnd-vahn-dring*
May I take photographs?	Får jag fotografera? *for-rr yuh foo-too-grruh-fea-rruh*

Planning

Do you have a guide-book/map of ...?	Har ni en resehandbok/karta över ...? *hahrr ni ehn rrea-seh-huhnd-book/kah-rtuh er-vehrr ...*
What are the main attractions?	Vilka är huvudattraktionerna? *vilk-uh air hü-vud-uht-rruhk-fhoon-ehrr-nuh*
May I take photographs?	Får jag fotografera? *for-rr yuh foo-too-grruh-fea-rruh*

🔍 : LOOK FOR

STRAND	**BEACH**
SLOTT	**CASTLE**
DOMKYRKA	**CATHEDRAL**
KYRKA	**CHURCH**
MONUMENT	**MONUMENT**
RUINER	**RUINS**

Questions

What is that?	Vad är det? vuh air *dea*
How old is it?	Hur gammal är den? hurr *guhm*-muhl *air* dehn

Getting In

What time does it open/ close?	När öppnar/ stänger de? hurr *duhks erp*-nuhrr/ *stehng*-ehrr dom

Fast Talk

Forming Sentences

You don't need to memorise complete sentences; instead, simply use key words to get your meaning across. For example, you might know that när *nair.* means 'when' in Swedish. So if you've arranged a tour but don't know what time, just ask *När är nästa avgång?* near air *nehs*-ta *av*-gong?. Don't worry that you're not getting the whole sentence right – people will understand if you stick to the key words.

Tours

Can you recommend a boat trip?	Skulle du kunna rekommendera en bra båttur?
	skul-leh du ku-nah re-ko-men-*dey*-ra ein brah *boht*-türr
Can you recommend a day trip?	Skulle du kunna rekommendera en dagsutflykt?
	skul-leh du ku-nah re-ko-men-*dey*-ra ein *dahgs*-üt-flewkt
Can you recommend a tour?	Skulle du kunna rekommendera en rundvandring?
	skul-leh duh ku-nah re-ko-men-*dey*-ra ein *ründ*-hvahn-dring

How much does it cost to get in?	Hur mycket kostar det i inträde?
	hurr mük-keh *kos*-tuhrr deh ee *in*-trrair-deh
Is there a reduction for students/children?	Finns det studentrabatt/barnrabatt?
	fins deh stu-dehnt-rruh-buht/bahrn-rruh-buht

Shopping

Fast Phrases

How much is it?	Hur mycket kostar det? *hurr mük-keh kos-tuhrr deh*
It's too expensive.	Det är för dyrt. *deh air fer-rr dürt*
Can I look at it?	Får jag se den? *fawr yaa se deyn*

In the Shop

I'm looking for ...	Jag letar efter ... *yaa ley·tar ef·ter ...*
I'd like to buy ...	Jag skulle vilja ha ... *yuh sku-leh vil-yuh hah ...*
Do you have others?	Har ni några andra andra? *hahrr ni nor-rruh uhn-drruh*
Can I look at it?	Får jag se den? *fawr yaa se deyn*
I (don't) like it.	Jag tycker (inte) om den/det. *yuh tük-kehrr (in-teh) om dehn/deh*
I'm just looking.	Jag tittar bara. *yuh tit-tuhrr bah-rruh*

Local Knowledge   Shops

Where would you go for bargains?	Var skulle du gå för att fynda? *vahrr skul-leh du go fer at fün-dah*
Where would you go for souvenirs?	Var kan man köpa souvenirer? *vahrr kan mahn choh-pah sou-ve-ni-rer*

It doesn't fit.	Den passar inte. *dehn puhs-uhrr in-teh*

Paying & Bargaining

Can you write down the price?	Kan du skriva ner priset? *kuhn doo skrree-vuh nearr prree-seht*
Do you accept credit cards?	Tar ni kreditkort? *tahrr ni krreh-deet-koort*
Could you lower the price?	Kan du gå ner i pris? *kuhn du gor nearr i prrees*
How much is it?	Hur mycket kostar det? *hurr mük-keh kos-tuhrr deh*

Souvenirs

earrings	örhängen	*er-rr-hehng-ehn*
glassware	glas	glahs
handicraft	hemslöjd	*hehm-sleyd*
necklace	halsband	*huhls-buhnd*

57

pottery	keramik	cheh-rruh-*meek*
ring	ring	*rring*

Clothes & Shoes

bathers	baddräkt/ badbyxor f/m	*bahd-drrehkt/* *bahd-bük-sorr*
clothing	kläder	*klae-dehrr*
coat	kappa/rock f/m	*kuhp-puh/rrok*
dress	klänning	*klehn-ning*
jacket	jacka	*yak-kuh*
jumper (sweater)	tröja	*trrer-yuh*
shirt	skjorta	*fhoo-rtuh*
shoes	skor	*skoorr*
skirt	kjol	*chool*
trousers/pants	byxor	*bük-ser*

Sizes & Comparisons

small	liten	*lee-tehn*
big	stor	*stoorr*

PHRASE BUILDER

It's too ...	Den är för ...	dehn air fer-rr ...
big/small	stor/liten	*stoorr/lee-tehn*
long/short	lång/kort	*long/kort*
loose/tight	vid/trång	*veed/trrong*

heavy	tung	tung
just right	lagom	*lah-gom*
light (not heavy)	lätt	leht
more	mer	mearr
less	mindre	*min-drreh*
too much/ many	för mycket/ många	fer-rr *mük-keh/ mong-uh*
many	många	*mong-uh*
enough	tillräckligt	*til-rrehk*-lit
also	också	*ok-so*
a little bit	lite grand	*lee*-teh *grruhn*

Colours

black	svart	svuhrt
blue	blå	blor
brown	brun	brrün
green	grön	grrern
orange	orange	o-*rruhnsh*
pink	rosa/skär	*rror*-suh/fhaer
purple	lila	*lee*-luh
red	röd	rrerd
white	vit	veet
yellow	gul	gül

Toiletries

comb	kam	kuhm
condoms	kondomer	kon-*dor*-mehrr
deodorant	deodorant	dea-oo-doo-*rruhnt*

hairbrush	hårborste	*hor-rr-bosh-teh*
moisturising cream	hudkräm	*hüd-krrairm*
mosquito repellent	myggolja	*müg-ohl-yuh*
razor	rakhyvel	*rrahk-hü-vehl*
razor blades	rakblad	*rrahk-blahd*
sanitary napkins	dambindor	*dahm-bin-der*
shampoo	schampo	*fham-poo*
shaving cream	raktvål	*rrahk-tvorl*
soap	tvål	tvorl
sunblock cream	solkräm	*sool-krrairm*
tampons	tamponger	tuhm-*pong*-ehrr
tissues	näsdukar	*nairs-dü-kuhrr*
toilet paper	toalettpapper	too-uh-*leht-puh*-pehrr
toothbrush	tandborste	*tuhn-bosh-teh*

Entertainment

Fast Phrases

What's on tonight?	Vad händer ikväll? vuh *haen*-derr e-kvael
What are your interests?	Vad har du för intressen? vuh hahrr du fer-rr in-*trrehs-sehn*
When/Where shall we meet?	Var ska vi träffas? varr skah vi *trea*-fas

Going Out

What's there to do in the evenings?	Vad finns det att göra på kvällarna? vuh fins deh uht *yer*-rruh po *kvehl*-luhrr-*nuh*
Are there places where you can hear Swedish folk music?	Finns det något ställe där man kan höra svensk folkmusik? fins deh not *stehl-leh* daer muhn kuhn *her*-rruh *svehnsk folk*-mu-*seek*
How much does it cost to get in?	Hur mycket kostar det i inträde hurr *mük*-keh *kos*-tuhrr deh ee in-*trrair*-deh

BIO	**CINEMA**
KONSERT	**CONCERT**
DISKOTEK	**DISCOTHEQUE**
NATTKLUBB	**NIGHTCLUB**
TEATER	**THEATRE**

Sports & Interests

What sports do you play?	Vilka sporter utövar du?	vil-kuh *spo-rtehrr* üt-er-vuhrr du
What are your interests?	Vad har du för intressen?	vuh hahrr du fer-rr in-*trrehs-sehn*

PHRASE BUILDER

I like ...	Jag tycker om ...	yuh tük-kehrr *om* ...
art	konst	konst
dancing	dans	duhns
football	fotboll	*foot-boll*
music	musik	mu-*seek*
reading	att läsa	uht *lair-suh*
travelling	att resa	uht *rrea-suh*

Hobbies

basketball	basket	*bahs*-keht
canoeing	att paddla kanot	uht *puh*-dluh kuh-*noot*
chess	schack	fhuhk

Festivals

Perhaps the most exotic of all Swedish festivals, Midsommar (Midsummer) is celebrated all over the country. The maypole, majstången, decorated with leaves and flowers, is erected in an open space. People who have a traditional costume wear it, and girls wear wreaths of flowers in their hair. Everyone dances around the maypole and sings traditional songs until late into the night that never really goes beyond dusk.

collecting ...	Jag samlar ...	yuh *suhm*-luhrr ...
computer games	datorspel	*dah*-to-rr-*speal*
fishing	att fiska	uht *fis*-kuh
hiking/trekking	att vandra	uht *vuhn*-drruh
horse riding	att rida	uht *rree*-duh
ice hockey	ishockey	*ees*-hok-kü
martial arts	kampsporter	*kuhmp*-spo-rtehrr
meeting (new) friends	att träffa (nya) vänner	uht *trrehf*-fuh (*nü*-uh) *vehn*-nehrr
movies	film	film
photography	fotografering	foo-too-grruh-*fea*-rring
running	att springa/ jogga	uht *sprring*-uh/ *yog*-guh
sailing	att segla	uht *seag*-luh
shopping	att shoppa	uht *shop*-puh
skating	att åka skridskor	uht or-kuh *skrri*-sker
(downhill) skiing	att åka (slalom)/ skidor	uht or-kuh (*slah*-lom)/*fhee*-der

swimming	att simma/ bada	uht *sim-muh/ bah-duh*
tennis	tennis	*tehn*-nis
visiting friends	att gå hem till kompisar	uht gor *hehm* til *kom*-pi-suhrr
walking	att gå ut och gå	uht gor *üt* o *gor*

Meeting up

When/Where shall we meet?	Var ska vi träffas? varr skah vi *trea*-fas
Let's meet at ...	Vi kan träffas vid ... ve kan *trea*-fas vid ...

Practicalities

⟹ Fast Phrases

Where are the toilets?	Var är toaletten? vahrr air too-uh-*leht*-tehn
Can I access the Internet from here?	Kan jag koppla upp mig på Internet härifrån? *kuhn* yuh kop-luh *up* may por *in*-tehrr-neht *haer*-i-frrorn
Where is the police station?	Var är polisstationen? vahrr air poo-*lees*-stuh-*fhoo*-nehn

Banking

I want to exchange some money.	Jag skulle vilja växla pengar. yuh *skul*-leh vil-yuh *vehks*-luh *pehng*-uhrr
What is the exchange rate?	Vad är växelkursen? vuh air vehks-ehl-ku-shehn
How many kronor per dollar?	Hur många kronor per dollar? hurr mong-uh *krroo*-ner parr *dol*-luhrr

BANKOMAT	**ATM**
UTLÄNDSK VALUTA	**FOREIGN EXCHANGE**
KASSA/KASSÖR	**CASHIER**

Phone/Mobile Phone

Can I use the telephone, please?	Kan jag få låna telefonen? kuhn *yah* fo *lor*-nuh teh-leh-*for*-nehn
I want to ring ...	Jag vill ringa till ... yuh vil *rring*-uh til ...
The number is ...	Numret är ... *num*-rreht air ...
How much does a three-minute call cost?	Hur mycket kostar ett treminuterssamtal? hurr mük-keh *kos*-tuhrr eht *trrea*-mi-*nü*-tehsh-suhm-*tahl*
How much does each extra minute cost?	Hur mycket kostar varje extra minut? hurr mük-keh *kos*-tuhrr *vuhrr*-yeh *ehks*-trruh mi-*nüt*
I'd like to speak to (Göran Persson).	Jag skulle vilja tala med (Göran Persson). yuh *skul*-leh vil-yuh *tah*-luh meh (yer-rruhn *pae*-shon)
I want to make a reverse-charges phone call.	Jag skulle vilja gör ett ba-samtal. yuh *skul*-leh vil-yuh *yer*-rruh eht *bea-ah*-suhm-*tahl*
What is the area code for ...?	Vad är riktnumret till ...? vuh air *rrikt-num*-rreht til ...

PRACTICALITIES

Understanding Swedish

Most sentences are composed of several words (or parts of words) serving various grammatical functions, as well as those that carry meaning (primarily nouns and verbs). If you're finding it hard to understand what someone is saying to you, listen out for the nouns and verbs to work out the context – this shouldn't be hard as they are usually more emphasised in speech. If you're still having trouble, a useful phrase to know is *Kan du vara snäll och tala lite långsammare?* kuhn du vuh snehl o tah-luh lee-teh long-suhm-muh-rreh? (Could you speak more slowly, please?).

It's engaged.	Det är upptaget. *deh air up-tah-geht*
I've been cut off.	Samtalet bröts. *suhm-tahl-eht brrerts*

Internet

Is there an internet cafe nearby?	Finns det något Internet-kafé i närheten? *fihns deh not in-tehrr-neht-kuh-fea i naer-hea-tehn*
Can I access the internet from here?	Kan jag koppla upp mig på Internet härifrån? *kuhn yuh kop-luh up may por in-tehrr-neht haer-i-frrorn*
I'd like to check my email.	Jag skulle vilja kolla min e-mail. *yuh skul-leh vil-yuh-kol-luh min ea-mail*

Emergencies

Help!	Hjälp! *yehlp*
Fire!	Elden är lös! *ehl*-dehn air *lers*
Thief!	Ta fast tjuven! tuh *fuhst* chü-vehn
Go away!	Försvinn!; Gå din väg! fer-*shvin*!; *gor* din *vairg*
Call the police!	Ring polisen! rring poo-*lee*-sehn
Where are the toilets?	Var är toaletten? vahrr air too-uh-*leht*-tehn
Could you help me please?	Kan du hjälpa mig? kuhn du *yehl*-puh *may*
It's an emergency!	Det är ett nödsituation! deh air ehn *nerd*-si-tu-uh-*fhoon*
There's been an accident!	Det har hänt en olycka! deh hahrr *hehnt* ehn oo-*lük*-kuh
Call a doctor/an ambulance!	Ring efter en doktor/ en ambulans! *rring* ehf-tehrr ehn *dok*-to-rr/ ehn uhm-boo-*luhns*
I'm lost.	Jag har gått vilse. yuh hahrr got *vil*-seh

Police

I've been raped.	Jag har blivit våldtagen. yuh hahrr got vil-seh *vold*- *tah*-gehn

I've been robbed!	Jag har blivit rånad! yuh hahrr blee-vit *rror-nuhd*
Where is the police station?	Var är polisstationen? vahrr air poo-*lees*-stuh-*fhoo*-nehn
I'll call the police!	Jag kallar på polis! yuh *kuhl*-luhrr po poo-*lees*
I wish to contact my embassy/consulate.	Jag vill kontakta min ambassad/mitt konsulat. yuh vil kon-*tuhk*-tuh min uhm-buh-*sahd*/mit kon-su-*laht*
Could I please use the telephone?	Kan jag få låna telefonen? kuhn yuh for *lor*-nuh teh-leh-*for*-nehn
I've lost my ...	Jag har förlorat ... yuh hahrr fer-*loo*-rruht ...
My possessions are insured.	Jag har försäkring. yuh hahrr fer-*shairk*-rring

PHRASE BUILDER

My ... was stolen.	Min ... har blivit stulen.	min ... hahrr blee-vit *stü-lehn*
bags	mina väskor	mee-nuh vehs-korr
handbag	min handväska	min huhnd-vehs-kuh
money	mina pengar	mee-nuh pehng-uhrr
travellers cheques	mina cheques resecheckar	mee-nuh rrea-seh-chehk-kuhrr
passport	mitt pass	mit puhs

I didn't do it.	Jag gjorde det inte. *yuh yoo*-rdeh deh *in-teh*
I'm sorry. I apologise.	Förlåt. Jag ber om ursäkt. fer-*lort*. yuh bearr om *ü-shehkt*
I didn't realise I was doing anything wrong.	Jag förstod inte att jag gjorde fel. yuh fer-*shtood* in-teh uht yuh yoo-rdeh *feal*

Health

I'm/My friend is sick.	Jag är/Min vän är sjuk. yuh air/min *vehn* air *fhük*
Could I see a female doctor?	Kan jag få träffa en kvinnlig läkare? kuhn yuh for *trrehf*-fuh ehn *kvin*-li *lair*-kuh-rreh
What's the matter?	Vad är det för fel på dig? vuh air deh fer-rr *feal* po *day*
Where does it hurt?	Var gör det ont? *vahrr* yer-rr deh *oont*
It hurts here.	Det gör ont här. deht yer-rr *oont haer*
I have ...	Jag har ... yuh hahrr ...

PHRASE BUILDER

Where is the ...?	Var är ...?	vahrr air ...
chemist	apoteket	uh-poo-*tea*-keht
dentist	tandläkaren	*tuhnd-lair*-kuh-rrehn
doctor	doktorn	*dok*-to-rn
hospital	sjukhuset	*fhük-hü*-seht

I have medical insurance.	Jag har sjukförsäkring. yuh hahrr *fhük-fer-shairk-rring*
I'm allergic to antibiotics/penicillin.	Jag är allergisk mot antibiotika/penicillin. yuh air uh-*lehrr*-gisk moot uhn-ti-bi-*or*-ti-kuh/pehn-i-si-*leen*
I'm pregnant.	Jag är gravid. yuh air grruh-*veed*
I'm on the pill.	Jag äter p-piller. yuh air-tehrr *pea-pil*-lehrr
I haven't had my period for ... months.	Jag har inte haft mens på ... månader. yuh hahrr *in*-teh huhft *mehns* por ... *mor*-nuh-dehrr
I have been vaccinated.	Jag är vaccinerad. yuh air vuhk-si-*nea*-rruhd
I have my own syringe.	Jag har min egen spruta. yuh hahrr min *ea*-gehn *sprrü-tuh*
I feel better/worse.	Jag mår bättre/sämre. yuh mor-rr *beht*-rreh/*sehm*-rreh

PHRASE BUILDER

I'm ...	Jag är ...	yuh air ...
asthmatic	astmatiker	uhst-mah-ti-kehrr
diabetic	diabetiker	dee-uh-bea-ti-kehrr
epileptic	epileptiker	eh-pi-lehp-ti-kehrr

Parts of the Body

ankle	vristen	*vrris*-tehn
arm	armen	*uhrr*-men
back	ryggen	*rrüg*-gehn
chest	bröstet	*brrerst*-eht
ear	örat	*er-rruht*
eye	ögat	*er-guht*
finger	fingret	*fing*-rreht
foot	foten	*foo*-tehn
hand	handen	*huhn*-dehn
head	huvudet	*hü-veht*
heart	hjärtat	*yarr-tuht*
leg	benet	*bea*-neht
mouth	munnen	*mun*-nehn
nose	näsan	*nair-suhn*
ribs	revbenen	*rreav-bea*-nehn
skin	huden	*hü*-dehn
stomach	magen	*mah-gehn*
teeth	tänderna	*tehn*-dehrr-nuh
throat	halsen	*huhl*-sehn
wrist	handleden	*huhnd-lea*-dehn

Ailments

an allergy	en allergi	ehn uh-lehrr-*gee*
a blister	en blåsa	ehn *blor-suh*
a burn	ett brännsår	eht *brrehn-sor-rr*
a cold	en förkylning	ehn fer-*chül*-ning
constipation	förstoppning	fer-*shtop*-ning

72

Body Language

Swedes aren't very different from other westerners when it comes to body language. They nod their head for yes and shake it for no. An inarticulate little uhuh or umh always means 'yes' and is often accompanied by nodding. 'No' is nej or nähä or a plain shake of the head without a sound.

You'll find that the Swedes will want to shake hands with you every time you meet, men and women alike. Kissing on the cheek is becoming more common among close friends, but the old hand shake is still the most common form of greeting.

a cough	hosta	*hoos-tuh*
diarrhoea	diarré	dee-uh-*rrea*
fever	feber	*fea*-behrr
headache	huvudvärk	*hü*-vud-*varrk*
hepatitis	hepatit/gulsot	heh-puh-*teet*/*gül-soot*
indigestion	dålig matsmältning	*dor*-li *maht-smehlt*-ning
an infection	en infektion	ehn in-fehk-*fhoon*
influenza	influensa	in-flu-*ehn*-suh
low/high blood pressure	lågt/högt blodtryck	*lorgt/hergt blood-trrük*
motion sickness	åksjuka	*ork-fhü*-kuh
sore throat	ont i halsen	ont i *huhl*-sehn
sprain	stukning	*stük-ning*
a stomachache	ont i magen	oont i *mah*-gehn
sunburn	solbränna	*sool-brrehn*-nuh

Useful Words

addiction	missbruk	*mis-brrük*
antiseptic	antiseptisk	*uhn-ti-sehp-tisk*
aspirin	magnecyl	*mang-neh-sül*
bandage	förband	*fer-rr-buhnd*
band-aid	plåster	*plos-tehrr*
a bite	ett bett	*eht beht*
blood pressure	blodtryck	*blood-trrük*
blood test	blodprov	*blood-prroov*
contraceptive	preventivmedel	*prreh-vehn-teev-mea-dehl*
injection	spruta	*sprrü-tuh*
injury	skada	*skah-duh*
itch	klåda	*klor-duh*
nausea	illamående	*il-luh-mor-ehn-deh*
panadol	panodil	*puh-noo-deel*
vitamins	vitaminer	*vi-tuh-mee-nehrr*
wound	sår	*sor-rr*

At the Chemist

I need medication for ...	Jag behöver ett medel mot ... *yuh beh-her-vehrr eht mea-dehl moot ...*
I have a prescription.	Jag har ett recept. *yuh hahrr eht rreh-sehpt*

At the Dentist

I have a toothache.	Jag har tandvärk. *yuh hahrr tuhnd-varrk*

I've lost a filling.	Jag har tappat en plomb.
	yuh hahrr *tuhp*-puht ehn *plomb*
I've broken a tooth.	Jag har slagit av en tand.
	yuh hahrr slah-git *ahv* ehn *tuhnd*
My gums hurt.	Jag har ont i tandköttet.
	yuh hahrr *oont* i *tuhnd-cher*-teht
I don't want it extracted.	Jag vill inte ha den utdragen.
	yuh vil *in*-teh hah dehn *üt-drrah*-gehn
Please give me an anaesthetic.	Jag vill ha bedövning.
	yuh vil hah be-*derv*-ning

Post

I'd like some stamps.	Jag skulle vilja ha några frimärken.
	yuh skul-leh vil-yuh *hah* nor-grruh *frree-marr*-kehn
How much does it cost to send this to ...?	Hur mycket kostar det att skicka det här till ...?
	hurr mük-keh *kos*-tuhrr deh uht *fhik*-uh deh *haer* til ...

PHRASE BUILDER

I'd like to send a ...	Jag skulle vilja skicka ett ...	yuh *skul*-leh vil-yuh *fhik*-kuh eht ...
letter	brev	*brreav*
postcard	vykort	*vü-koort*
parcel	paket	puh-*keat*

Dictionary

ENGLISH *to* SWEDISH

engelska – svenska

a

accommodation boende *boo-ehn-deh*

account konto *koh-ntoo*

aeroplane flygplan *flüg-plan*

afternoon eftermiddag *ehftehr-mid-duh*

air-conditioned luftkonditionering *lüft-kond-e-fhioo-neh-ring*

airport flygplats *flüg-plats*

airport tax flygplatsskatt *flüg-plats-skat*

alarm clock väckarklocka *vae-kar-kloh-kah*

alcohol alkohol *al-koo-hohl*

antique antikviteter *an-te-kve-tei-ter*

appointment möte *moh-teh*

arrivals ankomster *an-kom-sterr*

art gallery konsthall *kohnst-hal*

ashtray askkopp *ask-kohp*

at på/i *pae/e*

ATM bankomat *bank-oh-maht*

autumn höst *hust*

b

baby bebis *beh-bees*

back (body) rygg *rüg*

backpack ryggsäck *rüg-saek*

bad dåligt *doh-lit*

bag väska *vaeska*

baggage bagage *ba-gach*

baggage allowance bagagebidrag *ba-gach-bee-drag*

baggage claim förlorat bagage *fur-loh-rat ba-gach*

bakery konditori *kon-de-toh-ree*

Band-Aid plåster *ploh-ster*

bank bank *bank*

bank account bankkonto *bank-kohn-toh*

bath bad *bahd*

bathroom badrum *bahd-room*

battery batteri *bae-teh-ree*

beach strand *strahnd*

beautiful vacker *vah-kerr*

beauty salon skönhetssalong *fhun-hets-sa-long*

76

bed säng saeng
bed linen lakan lah-kan
bedroom sovrum sohv-room
beer öl erl
bicycle cykel sü-kel
big stor stoor
bill nota/räkning noo-ta/raek-neng
birthday födelsedag fu-dehl-seh-dag
black svart svart
blanket filt feelt
blood group blodgrupp blood-group
blue blå bloh
boarding house pensionat pen-fhio-nat
boarding pass boardingpass boarding-pas
boat båt boht
book bok book
book (make a booking) boka boo-kah
booked up full bokat full boo-kaht
bookshop bokaffär book-afaer
border gräns graens
bottle flaska flahska
box box box
boy pojke pohy-ke
boyfriend pojkvän pohyk-vaen
bra behå beh-hoh
brakes bromsar brom-sar
bread bröd brud
briefcase portfölj pohrt-fulj
broken sönder sun-der
brother bror broor
brown brun brün
building byggnad büg-nad
bus buss bus
bus station busstation bus-sta-fhion
bus stop busshållplats bus-hol-plats
business affär a-faer
business class förstaklass fur-sta-klas
busy upptagen oop-ta-gen
butcher's shop slaktarbutik slak-tar-booteek

cafe kaffé café
call ringa ree-nga
camera kamera kamrah
can (tin) burk buhrk
cancel avboka av-book-ah
car bil beel
car hire biluthyrning beel-üt-hür-ning
car owner's title bilägarens titel/namn beel-aeg-a-rens-tetehl
car registration bilregistrering beel-re-ji-ster
cash kontanter kon-tan-ter
cashier kassör/kassörska ka-surr/ka-surr-ska
chairlift (skiing) stollift stool-lift
change byta bü-tah
change (coins) mynt münt
change (money) växel vaek-sel
check titta te-ta
check (banking) check check
check-in (desk) checka in che-ka-in
cheque kontrollera kon-troh-le-rah
child barn barn
church kyrka chür-kah
cigarette lighter tändare taen-dah-reh
city stad stahd
city centre centrum cen-trum
clean ren rehn
cleaning att städa at stae-dah
cloakroom garderob gar-drob
closed stängt staengt
clothing kläder klae-deer
coat kappa kah-pah
coffee kaffe kah-fe
coins mynt münt
cold kallt kahllt
comfortable skönt fhunt
company sällskap sael-skahp
computer dator dah-toor
condom kondom kohn-dohm
confirm (a booking) konfirmera kohn-fer-meh-rah

77

connection förbindelse/anslutning fur-*ben*-del-se/*an*-slot-neng
convenience store närbutik naer-bootek
cook kock kok
cool cool kool
cough hosta hoostah
countryside landet *lan*-deht
cover charge kuvertavgift koo-*vert*-av-jift
crafts hantverk hant-verk
credit card kreditkort kreh-det-kort
currency exchange växelkurs vae-ksel-koors
customs tull tooll

d

daily dagligen *dahg*-le-gen
date datum *dah*-tom
date of birth födelsedatum *fu*-del-se-dag
daughter dotter doh-ter
day dag dahg
day after tomorrow (the) i övermorgon e *uver*-mor-gon
day before yesterday i förrgår e *fur*-gor
delay försenat fur-se-nat
delicatessen delikatessen de-li-ca-te-sen
depart avgång av-gong
department store varuhus va-ro-hos
departure avgång *av*-gong
deposit deposition deh-po-*si*-fhion
diaper blöja *blu*-ja
dictionary ordbok oord-book
dining car restaurangvagn restoo-*rang*-vagn
dinner kvällsmat kvaels-mat
direct direkt direct
dirty smutsigt *smot*-sigt
discount rabbatt ra-*bat*

dish disk disc
doctor doktor *doc*-tor
dog hund hoond
double bed dubbelsäng dob-al-seang
double room dubbelrum *dob*-al-room
dress klänning *klean*-ing
drink dricka *dre*-kah
drink (beverage) drink drink
drivers licence körkort kur-koort
drunk full full
dry torr tohr

e

each varje var-je
early tidigt *te*-degt
east öst ust
eat äta ea-ta
economy class standard *stan*-dard
elevator hiss his
embassy ambassad am-ba-*sad*
English engelska *eng*-ehl-ska
enough tillräckligt *til*-reak-ligt
entry entré entre
envelope kuvert ku-*vert*
evening kväll kveal
every varje var-je
everything allt alt
excess (baggage) överskott *u*-ver-skott
exchange byta *bü*-tah
exhibition utställning oot-*steal*-ning
exit utgång oot-gong
expensive dyrt dürt
express (mail) express ex-*press*

f

fall höst hust
family familj fam-*elj*
fare biljettpris bel-*het*-pres
fashion mode moo-deh
fast snabbt snab-t

father pappa/far papa/far
ferry färja *faer*-ja
fever feber *feh*-ber
film (for camera) filmrulle *felm*-ruhle
fine (penalty) böter *bu*-ter
finger finger *feng*-er
first class första klass *furs*-ta calss
fish shop fiskaffär *fesk*-af-aer
fleamarket loppis/loppmarknad *loh-pes/lohp*-mark-nad
flight flyg flüg
floor (storey) våning *voh*-ning
flu influensa in-flu-en-sa
footpath gångstig *gohng*-steg
foreign utländsk oot-leandsk
forest skog skoog
free (at liberty) fri free
free (gratis) gratis *gra*-tes
fresh fräscht frea-fht
friend kompis/vän *kom*-pes/vean

g

garden trädgård *trea*-gord
gas (for cooking) gas gas
gas bensin behn-*seen*
gift present preh-*sent*
girl flicka *fle*-ka
girlfriend flickvän *flekk*-vean
glasses (spectacles) glasögon *glas*-ugon
gloves handskar *hand*-skar
go gå goh
go out gå ut goh oot
go shopping shoppa chopa
gold guld goold
grateful tacksam *tuhk*-sam
gray grå groh
green grön grun
grocery matvaror *mat*-va-roar
guesthouse gästhus *geast*-hoos
guided tour guidetur guide-toor

h

half hälften healf-tehn
handsome snygg snüg
heated värmd vearmeh
help hjälp yealp
here här hear
highway motorväg *mo*-tor-veag
hire anställa *an*-stea-lah
holidays semester seh-*meh*-ster
honeymoon smekmånad *smek*-moh-nad
hospital sjukhus *fhuk*-hoos
hot varm varm
hotel hotell hoo-*tel*
hour timme *te*-meh
husband man man

i

identification legitimation leh-ge-te-ma-*fhion*
identification card (ID) legitimation leh-ge-te-ma-*fhion*
ill sjuk fhük
included inkluderat in-kloo-*deh*-rat
information information in-for-ma-*fhion*
insurance försäkring fur-*seak*-ring
intermission paus/avbrott paos/av-broht
internet cafe internet kaffé in-ter-*net* cafe
interpreter tolk tohlk
itinerary resväg/rutt rehs-veag/roott

j

jacket jacka ya-ka
jeans jeans yens
jewellery smycke *smü*-keh
journey resa reh-sa
jumper tröja tru-ya

k

key nyckel *nü*-kel
kind snäll snael
kitchen kök chuk

l

lane stig/väg steg/vaeg
large stor stoor
last (previous) Förgående *fur*-goh-ehn-deh
late sen sehn
later senare sehn-areh
launderette tvätteri tvaet-eree
laundry (clothes) smuttstvätt *smoots*-tveat
leather läder lae-der
leave gå goh
left luggage (office) kvarglömt kvar-glumt
letter brev brehv
lift Skjuts fhoots
linen (material) linne leneh
locked låst lohst
look for titta efter *te*-ta *ehf*-ter
lost borttappad *bort*-ta-pad
lost property office borttappat *bort*-ta-pat
luggage bagage ba-*gache*
luggage lockers bagageskåp ba-*gache*-skop
lunch lunch lunch

m

mail (postal system) post post
make-up smink smenk
man man man
manager (restaurant, hotel) arbetsledare *ar*-bets-*leh*-dareh
map (of country) karta kartah
map (of town) stadskarta stads-kartah

market marknad mark-nad
meal måltid *mohl*-teed
meat kött choht
medicine (medication) medicin/läkemedel meh-de-*sen*/lae-keh-meh-del
metro station tunnelbanestation *too*-nel-ba-neh-sta-*fhion*
midday middag *me*-dag
midnight midnatt med-*nat*
milk mjölk myulk
mineral water mineralvatten me-ne-*ral*-va-ten
mobile phone mobiltelefon moo-*bel*-teh-leh-*fone*
modem modem moh-*dem*
money pengar pae-ngar
month månad moh-nad
morning morgon mor-gon
mother mamma/mor mama/mohr
motorcycle motorcykel *mo*-tor-sü-kel
motorway motorväg *mo*-tor-veag
mountain berg baerj
museum museum mü-seh-oom
music shop musikaffär mü-*sik*-afaer

n

name namn namn
napkin servett ser-*vet*
nappy blöja *blu*-ya
newsagent tidningsaffär *teed*-nengs-af-aer
newspaper tidning *teed*-neng
next (month) nästa (månad) naesta
nice bra/snäll brah/snael
night kväll kvael
night out utekväll *oo*-teh-kvael
nightclub nattklubb *nat*-klub
no vacancy inga lediga rum eng-ah *leh*-de-ga room
non-smoking rökfritt ruk-freet
noon middag *me*-dag
north norr nor

now nu noo
number nummer *noo*-mer

o

office kontor kon-*toor*
oil olja *ol*-ya
one-way ticket enkelbiljett en-kehl-bel-*yet*
open öppet *uh*-pet
opening hours öppetider *uh*-peh-tee-der
orange (colour) orange oh-ranch
out of order fungerar ej fun-ge-rar ey

p

painter målare *moh*-lare
painting (a work) målar moh-lar
painting (the art) tavla ta-vla
pants byxa bü-ksa
pantyhose strumpbyxor stromp-bü-ksor
paper papper pa-per
party fest fehst
passenger ressenär re-seh-*naer*
passport pass pas
passport number passnummer pas-noo-mer
path väg vaeg
penknife pennkniv *penn*-kneev
pensioner pensionär pen-fhio-*naer*
performance föreställning fu-reh-*stael*-neng
petrol bensin ben-*seen*
petrol station bensinstation ben-seen-sta-fhion
phone book telefonbok te-leh-*fon*-book
phone box telefonkiosk te-leh-*fon*-chi-osk
phone card telefonkort te-leh-*fon*-kort
phrasebook parlör par-lur

picnic picknick pic-nic
pillow huvudkudde huh-vuhd-koo-de
pillowcase kuddfodral kuhd-foo-dral
pink rosa roh-sa
platform spår spohr
play (theatre) pjäs pyaes
police officer polisman poh-*les*-man
police station polisstation poh-*les*-sta-fhion
post code postnummer post-nuh-mer
post office posten poh-sten
postcard vykort vü-kort
pound (money, weight) Pund (£) puhnd
prescription recept re-*sept*
present presentera pre-sen-teh-ra
price pris prees

q

quick snabb snab

r

receipt kvitto *kvee*-too
red röd rud
refund återbetalning *oh*-ter-beh-tal-ning
rent hyra hü-ra
repair reparation re-pa-ra-*fhion*
retired har gått i pension har goht e pen-fhion
return lämna tillbaka laem-na teel-ba-ka
return (ticket) returbiljett re-*toor*-be-ljet
road väg vaeg
robbery rån rohn
room rum room
room rum room
room number rumsnummer rooms-nuh-mer
route väg vaeg

s

safe säker sae-ker
sea hav haav
season säsong seh-*song*
seat (place) säte/plats *sae*-te/plats
seatbelt säkerhetsbälte saeker-hets-bael-teh
self service självbetjäning *fhaelv*-be-chae-ning
service service ser-*vis*
service charge serviceavgift *ser*-vis-av-yift
share dela deh-la
shirt skjorta fhor-ta
shoe sko skoo
shop affär a-faer
shopping centre varuhus va-roo-hoos
short (height) kort kort
show visa (to show something)/föreställning visa
shower dusch duch
sick sjuk fhük
silk silke sel-ke
silver silver silver
single (person) singel singel
single room enkelrum *ehn*-kel-room
sister syster *süs*-ter
size (general) storlek *stoor*-lek
skirt kjol chol
sleeping bag sovsäck sohv-saek
sleeping car sovvagn sohv-vagn
slide (film) bild beld
smoke rök ruk
snack mellanmål me-lan-mohl
snow snö snoh
socks strumpor strump-or
son son sohn
soon snart snart
south syd süd
spring (season) vår vohr
square (town) torg tohry
stairway trappa tra-pa

stamp frimärke free-maer-ke
stationer's (shop) tidningsaffär *teed*-nengs-a-faer
stolen stulen stoo-len
stranger främling *fraem*-ling
street gata ga-ta
student student stoo-dent
subtitles undertexter oon-der-teks-ter
suitcase resväska *res*-vaeska
summer sommar soh-mar
supermarket mataffär mat-a-faer
surface mail ytpost üt-post
surname efternamn ef-ter-namn
sweater tröja tru-ya
swim simma see-ma
swimming pool pool pool

t

tall lång lohng
taxi stand taxihållplats taxi-*hol*-plats
teller kassör ka-ser
ticket biljett bel-*jet*
ticket machine biljettautomat bel-*jet*-auto-mat
ticket office biljettkontor bel-*jet*-kon-tor
time tid teed
timetable tidtabell *teed*-ta-bel
tip (gratuity) dricks dreks
to till tel
today idag e-dag
together tillsammans tel-sa-mans
tomorrow i morgon e mor-gon
tour tur tür
tourist office turistbyrå tür-*est*-bü-roh
towel handduk hand-dook
town stad staad
train station tågstation/järnvägsstation tohg-sta-*fhion*/jaern-veag-sta-fhion
transit lounge väntrum vaent-room

travel agency resebyrå res-bü-*roh*
travellers cheque resecheck res-chek
trip resa re-sa
trousers byxor bü-ksor
twin beds dubbelrum *du*-bell-room

u

underwear underkläder *un*-der-klae-der

v

vacancy lediga rum/lediga tjänster (work) leh-de-ga room/leh-de-ga chaen-ster
vacant ledig leh-deg
vacation semester se-*meh*-ster
validate validera va-lee-*de*-ra
vegetable grönsak grun-sak
view utsikt uht-seekt

w

waiting room väntrum vaent-room
walk gå goh
warm varm varm
wash (something) att tvätta något at *tvae*-ta noh-got

washing machine tvättmaskin *tveat*-ma-fhin
watch tvätta *tvea*-ta
water vatten va-ten
way väg veag
week vecka veh-ka
west väst vaest
what vad vuh
when när naar
where var vahrr
which vilken vel-ken
white vit veet
who vem vem
why varför var-fur
wife fru fruh
wifi wifi wi-fi
window fönster *fun*-ster
wine vin veen
winter vinter *ven*-ter
without utan uh-tan
woman kvinna kve-na
wool ull uhl
wrong (direction) fel (väg) fel (veag)

y

year år ohr
yesterday igår e-*gor*
youth hostel vandrarhem van-drar-hem

Dictionary

SWEDISH *to* ENGLISH

svenska – engelska

a

affär a-faer business/shop
alkohol al-koo-hohl alcohol
allt alt everything
ambassad am-ba-sad embassy
ankomster an-kom-sterr arrivals
anställa an-stea-lah hire
antikviteter an-te-kve-tei-ter antique
år ohr year
arbetsledare ar-bets-leh-dareh manager (restaurant, hotel)
askkopp ask-kohp ashtray
äta ea-ta eat
återbetalning oh-ter-beh-tal-ning refund
att städa at stae-dah cleaning
att tvätta något at tvae-ta noh-got wash (something)
avboka av-book-ah cancel
avgång av-gong depart/departure

b

bad bahd bath
badrum bahd-room bathroom
bagage ba-gach baggage/luggage
bagagebidrag ba-gach-bee-drag baggage allowance
bagageskåp ba-gache-skop luggage lockers
bank bank bank
bankkonto bank-kohn-toh bank account
bankomat bank-oh-maht ATM
barn barn child
båt boht boat
batteri bae-teh-ree battery
bebis beh-bees baby
behå beh-hoh bra
bensin behn-seen gas/petrol
bensinstation ben-seen-sta-fhion petrol station
berg baerj mountain
bil beel car

84

bilägarens titel/namn beel-aeg-a-rens-tetehl car owner's title
bild beeld slide (film)
biljett bel-*jet* ticket
biljettautomat bel-*jet*-auto-mat ticket machine
biljettkontor bel-*jet*-kon-tor ticket office
biljettpris bel-*het*-pres fare
bilregistrering beel-re-*ji*-ster car registration
biluthyrning beel-üt-hür-ning car hire
blå bloh blue
blodgrupp blood-group blood group
blöja blu-ja diaper/nappy
boardingpass boarding-pas boarding pass
boende boo-ehn-deh accommodation
bok book book
boka boo-kah book (make a booking)
bokaffär book-afaer bookshop
borttappad bort-ta-pad lost
borttappat bort-ta-pat lost property office
böter bu-ter fine (penalty)
box box box
bra/snäll brah/snael nice
brev brehv letter
bröd brud bread
bromsar brom-sar brakes
bror broor brother
brun brün brown
burk buhrk can (tin)
buss bus bus
busshållplats bus-*hol*-plats bus stop
busstation bus-sta-fhion bus station
byggnad *büg*-nad building
byta bü-tah change/exchange
byxa bü-ksa pants
byxor bü-ksor trousers

c

centrum cen-trum city centre
check check check (banking)

checka in che-ka-in check-in (desk)
cool kool cool
cykel sü-kel bicycle

d

dag dahg day
dagligen dahg-le-gen daily
dåligt doh-lit bad
dator dah-toor computer
datum dah-tom date
dela deh-la share
delikatessen de-li-ca-*te*-sen delicatessen
deposition deh-po-si-fhion deposit
direkt direct direct
disk disc dish
doktor doc-tor doctor
dotter doh-ter daughter
dricka dre-kah drink
dricks dreks tip (gratuity)
drink drink drink (beverage)
dubbelrum dob-al-room double room/twin beds
dubbelsäng dob-al-seang double bed
dusch duch shower
dyrt dürt expensive

e

eftermiddag ehftehr-mid-duh afternoon
efternamn ef-ter-namn surname
engelska eng-ehl-ska English
enkelbiljett en-kehl-bel-*yet* one-way ticket
enkelrum ehn-kel-room single room
entré entre entry
express ex-*press* express (mail)

f

familj fam-*elj* family
färja faer-ja ferry
feber feh-ber fever

fel (väg) fel (veag) wrong (direction)
fest fehst party
filmrulle felm-ruhle film (for camera)
filt feelt blanket
finger feng-er finger
fiskaffär fesk-af-aer fish shop
flaska flahska bottle
flicka fle-ka girl
flickvän flekk-vean girlfriend
flyg flüg flight
flygplan flüg-plan aeroplane
flygplats flüg-plats airport
flygplatsskatt flüg-plats-skat airport tax
födelsedag fu-dehl-seh-dag birthday
födelsedatum fu-del-se-dag date of birth
fönster fun-ster window
förbindelse/anslutning fur-ben-del-se/an-slot-neng connection
föreställning fu-reh-stael-neng performance
förgående fur-goh-ehn-deh last (previous)
förlorat bagage fur-loh-rat ba-gach baggage claim
försäkring fur-seak-ring insurance
försenat fur-se-nat delay
första klass furs-ta calss first class/business class
främling fraem-ling stranger
fräscht frea-fht fresh
fri free free (at liberty)
frimärke free-maer-ke stamp
fru fruh wife
full full drunk
full bokat full boo-kaht booked up
fungerar ej fun-ge-rar ey out of order

g

gå goh go/leave/walk
gå ut goh oot go out
gångstig gohng-steg footpath
garderob gar-drob cloakroom
gas gas gas (for cooking)

gästhus geast-hoos guesthouse
gata ga-ta street
glasögon glas-ugon glasses (spectacles)
grå groh gray
gräns graens border
gratis gra-tes free (gratis)
grön grun green
grönsak grun-sak vegetable
guidetur guide-toor guided tour
guld goold gold

h

hälften healf-tehn half
handduk hand-dook towel
handskar hand-skar gloves
hantverk hant-verk crafts
här hear here
har gått i pension har goht e pen-fhion retired
hav haav sea
hiss his elevator
hjälp yealp help
höst hust autumn
höst hust fall
hosta hoostah cough
hotell hoo-tel hotel
hund hoond dog
huvudkudde huh-vuhd-koo-de pillow
hyra hü-ra rent

i

i förrgår e fur-gor day before yesterday
i morgon e mor-gon tomorrow
i övermorgon e uver-mor-gon day after tomorrow (the)
idag e-dag today
igår e-gor yesterday
influensa in-flu-en-sa flu
information in-for-ma-fhion information
inga lediga rum eng-ah leh-de-ga room no vacancy

86

inkluderat in-kloo-*deh*-rat included

internet kaffé in-ter-*net* cafe internet cafe

j

jacka ya-ka jacket

jeans yens jeans

k

kaffe *kah*-fe coffee

kaffé café cafe

kallt kahlt cold

kamera kamrah camera

kappa kah-pah coat

karta kartah map (of country)

kassör ka-ser teller

kassör/kassörska ka-surr/ka-*surr*-ska cashier

kjol chol skirt

kläder *klae*-deer clothing

klänning *klean*-ing dress

kock kok cook

kök chuk kitchen

kompis/vän *kom*-pes/vean friend

konditori kon-de-toh-ree bakery

kondom kohn-*dohm* condom

konfirmera kohn-fer-*meh*-rah confirm (a booking)

konsthall *kohnst*-hal art gallery

kontanter kon-*tan*-ter cash

konto *koh*-ntoo account

kontor kon-*toor* office

kontrollera kon-troh-*le*-rah cheque

körkort kur-koort drivers licence

kort kort short (height)

kött choht meat

kreditkort kreh-det-kort credit card

kuddfodral kuhd-foo-dral pillowcase

kuvert ku-*vert* envelope

kuvertavgift koo-*vert*-av-jift cover charge

kväll kveal evening/night

kvällsmat kvaels-mat dinner

kvarglömt kvar-glumt left luggage (office)

kvinna kve-na woman

kvitto *kvee*-too receipt

kyrka *chür*-kah church

l

läder lae-der leather

lakan lah-kan bed linen

lämna tillbaka laem-na teel-*ba*-ka return

landet *lan*-deht countryside

lång lohng tall

låst lohst locked

ledig leh-deg vacant

lediga rum/lediga tjänster (work) leh-de-ga room/leh-de-ga chaen-ster vacancy

legitimation leh-ge-te-ma-*fhion* identification

legitimation leh-ge-te-ma-*fhion* identification card (ID)

linne leneh linen (material)

loppis/loppmarknad loh-pes/lohp-mark-nad fleamarket

luftkonditionering *lüft*-kond-e-fhioo-neh-ring air-conditioned

lunch lunch lunch

m

målar moh-lar painting (a work)

målare *moh*-lare painter

måltid *mohl*-teed meal

mamma/mor mama/mohr mother

man man husband

man man man

månad moh-nad month

marknad mark-nad market

mataffär mat-a-faer supermarket

matvaror *mat*-va-roar grocery

medicin/läkemedel meh-de-*sen*/lae-keh-meh-del medicine (medication)

mellanmål me-lan-mohl snack
middag *me*-dag midday/noon
midnatt med-*nat* midnight
mineralvatten me-ne-*ral*-va-ten mineral water
mjölk myulk milk
mobiltelefon moo-*bel*-teh-leh-*fone* mobile phone
mode moo-deh fashion
modem moh-*dem* modem
morgon mor-gon morning
möte *moh*-teh appointment
motorcykel mo-tor-*sü*-kel motorcycle
motorväg *mo*-tor-veag highway/ motorway
museum mü-*seh*-oom museum
musikaffär mü-*sik*-afaer music shop
mynt münt change (coins)

n

namn namn name
när naar when
närbutik naer-bootek convenience store
nästa (månad) naesta next (month)
nattklubb *nat*-klub nightclub
norr nor north
nota/räkning noo-ta/raek-neng bill
nu noo now
nummer *noo*-mer number
nyckel nü-kel key

o

öl erl beer
olja *ol*-ya oil
öppet *uh*-pet open
öppetider *uh*-peh-tee-der opening hours
orange oh-ranch orange (colour)
ordbok oord-book dictionary
öst ust east
överskott *u*-ver-skott excess (baggage)

p

på/i pae/e at
pappa/far papa/far father
papper pa-per paper
parlör par-lur phrasebook
pass pas passport
passnummer pas-noo-mer passport number
paus/avbrott paos/av-broht intermission
pengar pae-ngar money
pennkniv *penn*-kneev penknife
pensionär pen-fhio-*naer* pensioner
pensionat pen-fhio-nat boarding house
picknick pic-nic picnic
pjäs pyaes play (theatre)
plåster *ploh*-ster Band-Aid
pojke *pohy*-ke boy
pojkvän *pohyk*-vaen boyfriend
polisman poh-*les*-man police officer
polisstation poh-*les*-sta-fhion police station
pool pool swimming pool
portfölj pohrt-*fulj* briefcase
post post mail (postal system)
posten poh-sten post office
postnummer post-nuh-mer post code
present preh-*sent* gift
presentera pre-sen-*teh*-ra present
pris prees price
Pund (£) puhnd pound (money, weight)

r

rabbatt ra-*bat* discount
rån rohn robbery
recept re-*sept* prescription
ren rehn clean
reparation re-pa-ra-*fhion* repair
resa reh-sa journey
resa re-sa trip
resebyrå res-bü-*roh* travel agency

resecheck res-chek travellers cheque
ressenär re-seh-naer passenger
restaurangvagn restoo-rang-vagn dining car
resväg/rutt rehs-veag/roott itinerary
resväska res-vaeska suitcase
returbiljett re-toor-be-ljet return (ticket)
ringa ree-nga call
röd rud red
rök ruk smoke
rökfritt ruk-freet non-smoking
rosa roh-sa pink
rum room room
rum room room
rumsnummer rooms-nuh-mer room number
rygg rüg back (body)
ryggsäck rüg-saek backpack

ß

säker sae-ker safe
säkerhetsbälte saeker-hets-bael-teh seatbelt
sällskap sael-skahp company
säng saeng bed
säsong seh-song season
säte/plats sae-te/plats seat (place)
semester seh-meh-ster holidays/vacation
sen sehn late
senare sehn-areh later
servett ser-vet napkin
service ser-vis service
serviceavgift ser-vis-av-yift service charge
shoppa chopa go shopping
silke sel-ke silk
silver silver silver
simma see-ma swim
singel singel single (person)
självbetjäning fhaelv-be-chae-ning self service
sjuk fhük ill
sjuk fhük sick

sjukhus fhuk-hoos hospital
skjorta fhor-ta shirt
skjuts fhoots lift
sko skoo shoe
skog skoog forest
skönhetssalong fhun-hets-sa-long beauty salon
skönt fhunt comfortable
slaktarbutik slak-tar-booteek butcher's shop
smekmånad smek-moh-nad honeymoon
smink smenk make-up
smutsigt smot-sigt dirty
smuttstvätt smoots-tveat laundry (clothes)
smycke smü-keh jewellery
snabb snab quick
snabbt snab-t fast
snäll snael kind
snart snart soon
snö snoh snow
snygg snüg handsome
sommar soh-mar summer
son sohn son
sönder sun-der broken
sovrum sohv-room bedroom
sovsäck sohv-saek sleeping bag
sovvagn sohv-vagn sleeping car
spår spohr platform
stad stahd city/town
stadskarta stads-kartah map (of town)
standard stan-dard economy class
stängt staengt closed
stig/väg steg/vaeg lane
stollift stool-lift chairlift (skiing)
stor stoor big/large
storlek stoor-lek size (general)
strand strahnd beach
strumpbyxor stromp-bü-ksor pantyhose
strumpor strump-or socks
student stoo-dent student
stulen stoo-len stolen
svart svart black

syd süd south
syster süs-ter sister

t

tacksam tuhk-sam grateful
tågstation/järnvägsstation tohg-sta-fhion/jaern-veag-sta-fhion train station
tändare taen-dah-reh cigarette lighter
tavla ta-vla painting (the art)
taxihållplats taxi-hol-plats taxi stand
telefonbok te-leh-fon-book phone book
telefonkiosk te-leh-fon-chi-osk phone box
telefonkort te-leh-fon-kort phone card
tid teed time
tidigt te-degt early
tidning teed-neng newspaper
tidningsaffär teed-nengs-af-aer newsagent/stationer's (shop)
tidtabell teed-ta-bel timetable
till tel to
tillräckligt til-reak-ligt enough
tillsammans tel-sa-mans together
timme te-meh hour
titta te-ta check
titta efter te-ta ehf-ter look for
tolk tohlk interpreter
torg tohry square (town)
torr tohr dry
trädgård trea-gord garden
trappa tra-pa stairway
tröja tru-ya jumper/sweater
tull tooll customs
tunnelbanestation too-nel-ba-neh-sta-fhion metro station
tur tür tour
turistbyrå tür-est-bü-roh tourist office
tvätta tvea-ta watch
tvätteri tvaet-eree launderette
tvättmaskin tveat-ma-fhin washing machine

u

ull uhl wool
underkläder un-der-klae-der underwear
undertexter oon-der-teks-ter subtitles
upptagen oop-ta-gen busy
utan uh-tan without
utekväll oo-teh-kvael night out
utgång oot-gong exit
utländsk oot-leandsk foreign
utsikt uht-seekt view
utställning oot-steal-ning exhibition

v

väckarklocka vae-kar-kloh-kah alarm clock
vacker vah-kerr beautiful
vad vuh what
väg vaeg path/road/route
väg veag way
validera va-lee-de-ra validate
vandrarhem van-drar-hem youth hostel
våning voh-ning floor (storey)
väntrum vaent-room transit lounge/waiting room
var vahrr where
vår vohr spring (season)
varför var-fur why
varje var-je each/every
varm varm hot/warm
värmd vearmeh heated
varuhus va-ro-hos department store/shopping centre
väska vaeska bag
väst vaest west
vatten va-ten water
växel vaek-sel change (money)
växelkurs vae-ksel-koors currency exchange
vecka veh-ka week
vem vem who
vilken vel-ken which

vin *veen* wine
vinter *ven*-ter winter
visa (to show something)/
föreställning *visa* show
vit *veet* white
vykort *vü*-kort postcard

w

wifi wi-fi wifi

y

ytpost *üt*-post surface mail

Acknowledgments
Associate Product Director Angela Tinson
Product Editor Sandie Kestell
Language Writers Anna Herbst, Ida Burguete Holmgren, Pär Sörme
Cover Designer Campbell McKenzie
Cover Researcher Wibowo Rusli

Thanks
Kate Chapman, Gwen Cotter, James Hardy, Indra Kilfoyle, Genna
Patterson, Juan Winata

Published by Lonely Planet Global Ltd
CRN 554153

1st Edition – Jun 2018
Text © Lonely Planet 2018
Cover Image Stortorget square in Stockholm's Gamla Stan district,
Maurizio Rellini/4Corners©

Printed in China 10 9 8 7 6 5 4 3 2 1

Contact lonelyplanet.com/contact

Index

10. Phrases to Get You Talking

Hello.	Hej. *hay*
Goodbye.	Adjö!/Hej då! *uh-yer/hay dor*
Please.	Tack. *tuhk*
Thank you.	Tack. *tuhk*
Excuse me.	Ursäkta mig. *ü-shehk-tuh may*
Sorry.	Förlåt. *fer-lort*
Yes.	Ja. *yah*
No.	Nej. *nay*
I don't understand.	Jag förstår inte *yuh fer-shtor-rr in-teh*
How much is it?	Hur mycket kostar det? *hurr mük-keh kos-tuhrr deh*